SLAYING THE ONION

PRAISE FOR SLAYING THE ONION

Not only will you learn a refreshing, fun and comprehensive process of how to run a business, but you will fall in love with the author because of her authenticity and rawness; she is a true leader in the coaching industry.

~Becky Evans
Executive Leadership Coach

With over 35 years of working with human behavior, I am always looking for fresh material where I can gain insights. I will admit, when I pick up most books, I scan them and find most are a "rehash" of previous thought, not new challenging content. As I read, *Slaying The Onion*, I found myself reading and discovering fresh thoughts that made me stop, think and ponder. April has done an excellent job of reaching from her journey to share with us steps that will release us from the prison we make ourselves a hostage to. You will find thought provoking ideas, a journey that will feed your spirit and open you to pondering new life altering information. Great job April!

~Richard Flint, CSP
Author, *The Truth About Stress*
RichardFlint.com

If you have ever wondered why you sometimes make poor choices, April's *Slaying the Onion* will help you discover your hidden drivers. I have known April for several years and have worked with her both individually and with my team. She has consistently delivered amazing insight, inspiration, guidance and value. This book will enable you to also benefit from her skills and expertise.

Richard Hall
BottomLine Lawyers

Having just tasted a small slice of what was written [in *Slaying the Onion*] I saw the truth in your words without a sliver of mumbo-jumbo. You explained it all so well that even a knucklehead could understand. Thank you, April, for your hard work and dedication to helping others, myself included.

~David R. Gregory
News Director/News Anchor, 103.9 The Fish

Looking back on my life, I realize that some of my biggest mistakes were made through naivety and a lack of honesty with myself. In *Slaying the Onion*, leadership coach April Ballestero provides the tools and motivation to aid in honestly peeling back the layers of life in order to escape our self-created jail cells. With wisdom and gentleness, April guides the reader to discover the keys to unlock each layer of the onion—and ultimately, to escape the jail cell and experience true freedom.

Dr. Craig von Buseck
Managing Editor, *Inspiration.org*
Author, *Seven Keys to Hearing God's Voice*

SLAYING THE ONION

UNVEIL THE LAYERS OF YOUR STORY
TO REVEAL YOUR HIGHEST POTENTIAL

Dear Lisa,
Thank you for trusting
God to walk this
journey with us!

APRIL BALLESTERO

WordCrafts Press

Published by WordCrafts Press
Cody, Wyoming 82414
www.wordcrafts.net

To every precious soul that took the time to browse, read,
and deep dive into this book;
I am thankful to cross paths with you.

To every precious soul that took the time
to cross paths with me;
you have impacted my life. I thank you!

To a few specific souls who prefer to remain unnamed
(you know who you are!);
I thank you!

Most importantly, to the Master who allows me
to be a vessel and voice in His service;
I pray this book adds light and value across the globe!

Contents

WHY TRUST HER AWARENESS, CONCEPT, AND RESOURCES

When I first met April seven years ago, I was a newly licensed and hesitant real estate agent. April was teaching a class at the real estate brokerage I worked with at the time. Attending that class and meeting April changed the trajectory of my real estate career and my life. April presented many concepts and strategies that were completely new to me. At the end of the class, I decided to invest in myself and in my career and began formal coaching with April. Because April's style of coaching is comprehensive, I experienced growth in all areas of my life; business, family, spiritual, financial, and recreational. April asks the best questions! She has been instrumental in showing me how to be aware of my words, thoughts, actions, and habits and how these affect all areas of my life. Coaching with April took me from an insecure, fearful gal hoping to make a go of a real estate career to a successful business owner.

If I had not implemented the priceless advice, plans, and strategies April has shared with me over the years, I fully

1

believe I would have given up on my hopes and dreams of becoming a business owner. April is patient, kind, and extremely insightful. She draws from years of experience in the world of business, coaching—and being coached—and life. Those who have the opportunity to be coached by April or read her books will certainly be blessed and the better for it.

~Traci Harris
Real Estate Broker Associate, West Shores Realty

The conversation started simply enough. After all, it was just one of those get-to-know-you meetings—until our light banter turned intensely personal.

"My significant other expects me to fill their cup, every day!"

It soon became clear from the conversation that both individuals in that relationship had the same expectation for the other to completely meet all their needs, all the time, yet each saw the others flaws—flaws that kept them at an arm's length. I could guess the result before it was revealed. They decided they would be better off as *friends* than moving forward with a committed, long-term relationship.

These two had a wonderful opportunity to slay their onions, I thought. *Such a sad place they stay stuck in their comfort zones.*

This situation is not uncommon. It happens all the time in relationships, be they personal, business, family, or spiritual.

Think of the onion as being your heart, mind, and soul. While I'm not particularly skilled in the fields of psychology, biology—or any other -ology, for that matter—I am quite adept at asking questions, observing relationships, and facilitating unique methods for uncovering what is important to individuals. That's what slaying the onion is all about.

The decision to look in the mirror is not an easy one. Many people avoid it at all costs. I know. I fell into that trap for years. I was frightened, disappointed, and challenged by what I saw, so why bother looking?

One day my dance instructor observed me fidgeting with my blouse. "Stop that," he told me. "The mirror does not lie."

That simple truth made me realize how difficult it is to see yourself with all your imperfections. But you can't fix what you don't see.

Here is a fun example of a movie character sharing thoughts on onions.

Shrek: Ogres are like onions.
Donkey: They stink?
Shrek: Yes. No.
Donkey: Oh, they make you cry.
Shrek: No.
Donkey: Oh, you leave em out in the sun, they get all brown, start sproutin' little white hairs.
Shrek: No. Layers. Onions have layers. Ogres have layers. Onions have layers. You get it? We both have layers.
Donkey: Oh, you both have layers. Oh. You know, not everybody likes onions.

As Donkey shared in the wonderful movie *Shrek*. "Not everybody likes onions." True words. Onions might make you cry, but they might add flavor to an otherwise bland recipe. Whether you love 'em or hate 'em, one thing you can count on is, all onions are designed with layer upon layer upon layer.

Our goal is to make the process of *slaying the onion* easy to read, recommend, and register for in our online community. We will share more about this as we move forward.

Let's start by clarifying why this process is so important to your physical, mental, emotional, financial, and all the other health related conversations. What might you be hiding from? Weight gain? Alcohol dependency? Pornography? Maybe you simply suffer from a lack of inspiration or motivation. Whatever it is, you know it is eating away at your soul. And you're not alone. An enormous number of people all over the globe share these same challenges. How else do you explain why businesses like Costco and Sam's Club dramatically expanded their alcoholic beverage sections during the Covid-19 pandemic?

What we think we are hiding from, pushing down, or avoiding is eating away at our heart, mind, and soul. We live in a hurting world, one that tends to avoid facing the depth of emotion, the stories, and the life lessons that can set us free. The end result is we keep playing small. I know. I have been there, done that, and got the tshirt—quite a few of them actually. I have had to slay many of my own onions along the way. I will share my stories as we move along, as well as stories of my clients—with their permission, of course.

Thank you in advance for the trust. I hope to show you that you are far more valuable than the stuff that is attempting to hold you hostage to your old mindset—the stuff that keeps you chained to stories and beliefs that do not serve you. Together, if we are willing, we can face the tough layers of our lives.

We'll deep dive into the core of who we are. This is when we become BRAVE and courageous to BE our WHOLE self from the inside out.

The world, our parents, our teachers, and significant relationships in our life have taught us about reactionary response. We know how to respond to a social media post, a text, and even a phone call. We don't always know how to truly listen, show up in another person's world, and deeply hear, value, and see the person we are working to have a relationship with. This is where *Slaying the Onion* comes in. Our goal is for you to learn to commit, gain awareness, and share your true internal self from who you want to be, what you want to be responsible for, who you want to attract, what you want to value, and how you want people to experience you.

There is much more you will discover in our journey together, and I believe it will be worth your time and effort. It may not be simple. I guarantee it won't be easy. But if you commit to investing the time and energy, this journey will be worthwhile. My team and I are available to support your journey through the online course, videos, and community we have created to walk with you through the tough spots and celebrate the wins. Life is short. It's past time we get determined to slay the onions of our life, of our communities, and of our world ASAP!

WHAT IS SLAYING THE ONION?

My personal definition of *Slaying the Onion* means to know there are layers upon layers of fears, emotions, and stories worth facing and overcoming. We get to slay by *Defeating Our Fears!*

Ready to slay?

CHAPTER ONE

LOOKING IN THE MIRROR

"Maybe stories are just data with a soul."

~Brene Brown

We were in the middle of discussing the *Slaying the Onion* process during a group session, when a curious coaching client asked, "When you get stuck in the conversation, and you know the other person is resistant to going into the next layer of their onion, then what?" I realized her question was so profound, even while the group members were struggling to understand why they would even want to slay the layer without any motive or purpose. It was obvious to me then, she was ready to be an onion slayer. The onion development process actually originated when I realized so many did not know how to look in the mirror, face their fears, and challenge themselves and their so called comfort zone. Slaying is an intense process. It requires us to delve into our hearts, minds, and souls one layer at a time.

The problem is that we have all built walls around our

hearts that we believe offer protection. This is the outer layer of your onion. We have all created our own jail cells. The authentic voice and message locked inside those walls will never be heard without first knocking down those walls. Fortunately, we all have the key to start revealing both the light within and the light calling us to knock down those walls and step out of that cell.

The process I personally went through to discover the layer concepts—from What is on your Radar, to the WHOLE and BRAVE exercises, releasing the chains that were extreme obstacles to building the bridges for the Whole and Brave communication process—are all wrapped up in the next few chapters. We all have self created our own jail cell, and we have the key to start revealing the light within and the light calling us to step out of the cell.

It will take a process to unlock the reasons you have justified making those walls so thick, and it will take a process to start revealing the messages hiding inside your walls. You might think you have slain that onion layer and then be surprised when another layer emerges from beneath. Be prepared to give yourself grace and walk away from the experience for a season if need be. A good percentage of the population who buy this book may read a page or two, maybe even a chapter and decide, *I do not need this*, and move on. I am seeking the two percent who will complete every exercise, share and teach it to others, and let us know how it impacts those they get to serve.

My first life coach exposed me to the concept of conscious competence and unconscious competence. We all have items we *know* we know which is conscious competence. This is how we like our coffee, our times tables, and maybe even some basic English rules—like when a semicolon is used in a sentence. We also know what we *don't* know, which is conscious incompetence. Such as the reason others think the way they do or how my mind still forgets where I left my glasses that I just had on my head five minutes ago. These are known awareness. The unconscious competence is where the conscious mind goes into auto pilot and knows something so well, it just does without extreme thought of what needs to be done. On the other hand the unconscious mind in incompetence is where more often than not I get to work. Most people choose to work with me in what they know they don't know and realize there are so many additional opportunities. Thus, now I will walk you through the process I learned to start revealing the phases of the onion discovery process I went through to create and inspire Onion Slayers.

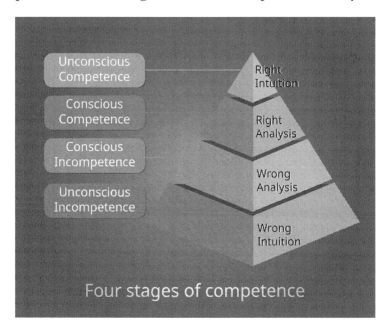

Four stages of competence

WHAT IS ON YOUR RADAR?

What does radar have to do with onions? It started actually as a dart board in my mind asking my clients what was their bullseye target for the day, month, year etc. Sadly, not everyone knew their answer. I had a multitude of tools in the business arena to ask about numbers, narrative plans, and overall business structures. What I discovered was that until each individual got clear about what their life wheel looked like, they were going through the motions. There are many versions of the life wheel, yet the one included will be a starting place to guide you through a very simple awareness tool. This will help us start to discover what is really on your radar.

Just like when you are driving on a highway, radar is what gives police officers the ability to hold drivers accountable to the speed limit. In many other situations, radar plays a part in assessing what is believed to be accurate and how it impacts everything else in the radar screen.

Example—A vehicle traveling at an alarming speed may also cause many challenges and even impact lives in some cases. For those of us who have a lead foot, it can result in speeding tickets, and we may learn to just attempt to not get caught next time.

I would not be completely vulnerable with you if I didn't share. I have had a few of these speeding tickets over the years—one even with my twin getting one at the same time. We were 19 years old flying down the 15 freeway in Southern Califonia from Victorville to Downey Califonia. It didn't matter that there was fog on the road and dangerous conditions. We were young and stupid. Obviously we were not paying attention to any radar concerns. I am positive we were not alone in these type of experiences. Thus, I started helping my clients learn they needed to create their own radar system. The development process, which started with a basic understanding of coaching has also gained its own layers as we move along.

Over the years working with my clients, the visual tool helps them realize what areas they are truly feeling fulfilled. Many have learned how to deeply appreciate the ability to measure where they are and how ridiculously balanced they are or are not. If you were brave enough to measure your own fulfillment on a scale from 1 to 10—10 being best, where

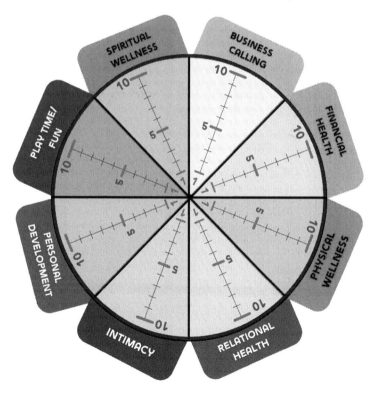

would you land in each area of the pie? By the way, if you are the type of person that needs to add some personalization to the process, feel free to change a subject, add pieces of the pie or whatever you like to make this your own. In all my years of coaching and training, you would be amazed at what I get to see, hear, and experience.

Another way we may want to contemplate this is to ask what energy or wealth are you experiencing in each of these areas of your life? Example—Financial health, for some, is something they are happy to address. They look at their financial statement everyday and are excited about how to add to the bottom line. Their number in this quadrant will be completely different than another person who hates to look at bank statements. They are wise to surround them-selves with people who keep them balanced in this area and help them learn how to appreciate it. Yet, fulfillment in this pie piece will be determined by a number of factors related to their perception and appreciation of their own financial awareness, in some cases training, and in many cases their beliefs around money.

For some the spiritual wellness pie piece is a very wealthy area for them in their belief of who or how they serve. You may have heard the phrase, "Where your treasure is, there is your heart." Ironically, this is a spiritual phrase with multiple meanings depending on who you are talking to. In each per-son's perception of their spiritual journey, a number may be determined on what impact they have in their area of service, how they feel personally about their personal relationship with the God they choose to serve. Again, so many other conversations available in this one slice.

As you are beginning to see, you get to decide your own

perception. You are your own expert. You get to look in that mirror one piece at a time. Remember this journey is for your benefit, not for beating up on yourself. We may never change the past, it is done! Remove any thoughts regarding this immediately. I know this is easier said than done. Although, what we keep on our eyes, heart, mind, and in our will expands, thus choosing where we align moving forward is where we want to take you.

For those of you who have actually taken the time to draw in the lines and connect them together to attempt to make your own circle, many will find a trapezoid or some figure you may not even know how to describe. This is ridiculously common. The even more challenging awareness is to determine that the wheels you just created are now the four wheels on the vehicle you drive every day. How is the drive? A tad bit bumpy? Are you able to drive at all? Many have found it is difficult to see where they are and what is possible to change what they now are aware of. You will hear this often—awareness is the first step.

The best immediate step is to decide where your strengths are and how you add value to the other areas of your wheel in small daily tangible options. Example: One of my strengths is to take daily spiritual wellness time to read, listen, and pray. This strength and discipline is an area I get to add value to my business calling.

Even this morning as I realized a way I did this when I first started as a coach had been overlooked. Now, I get to remember to ask, who does God want me to serve on this specific day?

Although, I had fallen short in many days in this area, it was part of my muscle memory I want to be more purposeful adding commitment to. It always amazes me when I apply, listen, and act on this nudging the conversations, connections, and clarity arise.

The decision is to determine whether you are willing to consider what is on your radar and do something about it. After spending years asking my clients what is on their radar in a multitude of ways, I realized I was hitting a multitude of brick walls. Most clients didn't even realize they were giving me such resistance. The terminology that then became normal was, *Let's peel a few of these layers.* Thus the "What is on your Radar" question became "How do we peel these layers?"

PEELING AND SLICING THE LAYERS

The year I first started as an executive coach I remember saying in an informal networking event, "I have a really good chisel" for those who have walls around their life, heart, and business. A chisel is used to cut or shave multiple metal, wood, or other products. For this journey, we are slaying the onions we all have—cutting into them with our sharpened knives is not that easily done for a human being. One of my clients actually asked me to help her slice her onion wide open. The moment she asked, I realized this is not the ideal way for some. In most cases, it requires a process to peel aways these layers. Thus a chef's knife would normally be ideal to cut all the way through, a paring knife will be more ideal for the process we are diving into.

The radar concept is just a step to help each person see the layers to peel or slice. This gives you a tool to determine and see the multiple areas of your life. Of course, as you start to see the areas you feel fulfillment in and the areas that are

14

lacking or ready for some improvement, this is where the difficulty arises. I am sure you may feel like many others who say, "I will deal with that someday." The layers we think are hidden or comfortable in the so-called *comfort zone* I will continuously refer to, bury circumstances, pain, and challenges so they do not impact our day-to-day life. The realization that if and when we are truly ready to take a look in the mirror and ask ourselves the hard questions—this is when we get to determine what a new life looks like.

Would you be interested in starting small? Maybe a question like, *In any of the areas of the radar we previously discussed, what would be one area you would choose first?* What would move the number you chose in this area one number up? Example: I chose a 4 in my physical wellness. I share this personally as I had gotten to the heaviest I have ever been in 2020. Of course, many of us have so many justifications, excuses for allowing ourselves to gain weight in the midst of a pandemic. The reality is for me, I was avoiding the ending of my fifth marriage.

Yes, I did say fifth.

I had some serious layers to relationships. For my legalistic friends, I know you don't mean to be judgmental, yet the Bible gives you authority to do so. I have already addressed this with God, counselors, and pastors, and I am forgiven. What I am also is a vessel for all who are reading that have also had one divorce, one failed relationship, or whatever caused you to gain weight at an overwhelming level.

I even went and created a podcast called *Addressing the Elephant in the Room* to help others, including myself, learn to speak up and communicate about the elephants in the room. It was a long list of items that caused me to start seeing the writing on the wall, and it was not until 2021 I was brave enough to move out. I finally dropped 12 pounds and got under 200 pounds in the first quarter of 2021 from the decision to start making myself a priority.

This moved me from level 3 to a 4 in my fulfillment of my health. I am overall healthy. I still run out of breath way too quickly, but so far I am overall down 26 pounds from the top weight. I have personally and professionally decided 10 more pounds will move me to a 5 and so on. I am committing to keep moving towards my healthy weight category by the end of 2021. That is a huge commitment and not recommended for many. I realized in order for me to be an example to others, I too get to lead the pack from my presence. I have 55 pounds to go. Sadly and joyfully, this will get me to the top of my height and weight categories and that will still be a huge win. Then I will still be at a 9 out of 10 in my health including other items because maintaining this health takes work. The emotional, mental, spiritual, physical and so much more all get to align.

Are you starting to see the depth of the layers we are slowly working through?

What does this mean for you to be slaying your onion? The layers you have to each category have been there a while. The decision to avoid them may have also been there a while. This is one of the many reasons I chose to write this book. As one publisher said to me when I was pitching this book, "Are you sure you want someone walking by themselves doing this work?" The first step is deciding you are willing to look in the mirror. In most cases, many have been asking you questions, planting seeds, and nudging you in some area of your life. You are really not alone as you think you are.

I have a team that manages my social media groups, my websites, etc. I feel this is a good time to invite you to connect with me online through the *Slaying the Onion* group page.

https://www.onelightacademy.com/courses/
slaying-the-onion-via-wordcrafts-press

Let me first say if you have some deep emotional, trauma, etc., we may direct you to some counseling resources, yet please do seek them out in your local area as well. Yet, if you are in a place where you are truly ready, then you are welcome to start the process of using the online platform with this book as well. Do any or all of it at your pace. We will be with you to encourage you, acknowledge your investment in yourself, and give you some thoughts and questions you may not have thought of specific to your unique situation. Just like peeling the layers, we have layers of services and products you are welcome to check out. Yet you are our first priority. The course online will have the same resources in this book and give you more video and written direction if you need or want it.

Quick reminder—layers have layers, which is how the WHOLE and BRAVE process we are moving into got created. Year after year, I realized people needed a way to start discerning and determining what is in each of these layers. Conversation after conversation, training after training, and wall after wall, I knew I had to find a way to help people see deeper into what their stories were telling them; without them having the ability to create roadblocks before they could uncover a part of themselves for their benefit.

It was not rocket science. Instead it was a scientific experiment that after 1000s of times proved consistently to reveal discoveries that always awed the client. The words and phrases have their own meanings that will get discussed as we move forward. The discovery of how these words worked so powerfully was also a unique process. Each person's trials and errors shared in coaching, decades of trials and tribulations of my own, all have revealed exercises that make an impact, including the one we are going into next.

In the following chapter, you will get exposed to ways to learn more about yourself in an unique way. You may also want to complete the exercise multiple times and multiple seasons as the answers do change. Yet, take the time to play along and discover what may surprise you and has surprised small business owners, heads of large organizations, to CEOs of multiple companies. It is worth your time. It will seem strange as you walk through the assignments and layers. Thank you, in advance, for showing up completely present in each chapter and journey.

SUMMARY

One final thought and a few more items to verify you are staying purposeful in becoming an onion slayer. The decision to become all you want to be, called to be, and committed to being is not an overnight process for most. Most, so-called *overnight successes* committed to the hard work day after day, night after night, and sacrifice after sacrifice. I am one of those people as well. I still do not claim to be successful because I wholeheartedly believe I am not done yet. My layers, my commitments, and the people I want to touch are still awaiting my moment by moment presence.

LIVING UNLAYERED CHAPTER ONE COMMITMENTS

- I choose to look in the mirror daily and I love who I see!
- I choose to assess what is on my radar/life wheel to know what is real!
- I choose to own one action, emotion, and thought on a daily basis to improve my wheel!
- I choose to give myself grace as I need it without beating up on myself.
- I choose to utilize my slaying principles one layer or half a layer at a time!
- I choose to understand as I slay each layer it may reveal another layer!
- I choose to engage in the Living Unlayered community to encourage and BE encouraged!

Chapter Two

The WHOLE Perspective

"Our minds influence the key activity of the brain, which then influences everything; perception, cognition, thoughts and feelings, personal relationships; they're all a projection of you."

~Deepak Chopra

The perceptions we create in our mind become our WHOLE reality. We get to put on a set of filters every day from our experiences and stories. These filters are like a magnifying glass you put on to engage and observe in each conversation and behavior. After years of asking questions, clarifying radar perceptions, words kept repeating in the questions. These words then became the layers and the WHOLE experience. This unique experience I am going to ask you to engage in is a tool to uncover expressions, beliefs, and revelations that may surprise you.

We will combine three overall explanations. The first explanation will be to share how this whole concept was created, documented, and proven in each section to consistently awe every person who participates in the experience.

This explanation will be after you complete the exercise so we don't take away from the layers you get to discover. The second explanation is to walk you through other stories and how they may resonate with you. Finally, each layer will have questions available to journal through this experience. The choice, clarity, and commitment of your forward movement is to put your discoveries into action. This action helps you continue your Living Unlayered journey.

THE WHOLE EXERCISE™

As we described, this exercise has been given, discussed, and delivered to audiences across the country. Each individual that takes the time to invest in being present for each part of the exercise finds the final product is quite intriguing. Sharing the exercise with your partners, family, team, or corporation without sharing your expectation of the end results is also very enlightening. Remember, perceptions are in the eye of the beholder, and when another hears, truly listens, and validates the gift to have perceptions, new communication gets formed.

This is now what you get to do for yourself. Remember the first part of the exercise is to answer each specific question in less than a minute with your instantaneous response. This immediate response will discover far more than you realize and help the end product have more authenticity. There is nothing needed to be polished or perfected in this exercise as it is just us. There is just one more clarity needed to help you truly understand the exercise.

Every word I give you needs two responses. The way the mind works it has two worlds: the external world you physically operate in, and the internal world your own perceptions, feelings and beliefs get created and experienced. As you see the word below, you will be asked to first give your immediate one word or phrase response to the word for the external world and then you will be given another line to answer from your own internal world. The external world is how you personally and professionally experience the outer world. The internal perspective is how you are personally and professionally experiencing your own unique internal world. The two do have completely different perspectives as you will discover.

It is easy to want to make this exercise complicated. The biggest obstacle is narrowing down to one word or phrase. It is all about the first word that comes to mind. The biggest gift you may give yourself is to not overthink it. Remember every word or phrase is completely from your perspective, no wrong or right answers, just about letting yourself see your own answers on paper. One additional reminder, in order to make this experience reveal the most value be sure to not pick the same word or phrase for any request. Example if you pick the word complex for any of these requests, make sure it is only picked once.

Here we go!

WHOLE EXPERIENCE™

Think about the word, *World*. What word will you choose to describe the word from an external perspective? My word would be *expansive* at this moment as I realize the world is quite expansive physically. Note: just write the word that comes to mind; no description is needed unless you want to journal your reasoning for later use.

Internal perspective would be developing due to the opportunities unfolding internally.

Let's now answer each one from an external perspective.

What word would you choose for WORLD from an external perspective?

Word is—

What word would you choose for HISTORY from an external perspective?

Word is—

What word would you choose for ORGANIZATION from an external perspective?

Word is—

What word would you choose for LOVE from an external perspective?

Word is—

What word would you choose for EXPERIENCE from an external perspective?

Word is—

Let's now answer each one from an internal perspective.

What word would you choose for WORLD from an internal perspective?

Word is—

What word would you choose for HISTORY from an internal perspective?

Word is—

What word would you choose for ORGANIZATION from an internal perspective?

Word is—

What word would you choose for LOVE from an internal perspective?

Word is—

What word would you choose for EXPERIENCE from an internal perspective?

Word is—

SUMMARIZING YOUR WHOLE EXPERIENCE EXTERNAL & INTERNAL

Now putting them all together for the final tasks of this exercise:

Re-write your words in the following space for external perspective:

World—

History—

Organization—

Love—

Experience—

By adding words or phrases, as many as you like, even if you create a run-on sentence, create a sentence with these words about your external WHOLE perspective.

Now, re-write your words in the following space for internal perspective:

World—

History—

Organization—

Love—

Experience—

Now, by adding words or phrases, as many as you like, even if you create a run-on sentence, create a sentence with these words about your external WHOLE perspective, then repeat the process to create a sentence about your internal WHOLE perspective.

External Sentence—

Internal Sentence—

The response I get from most, "How did this simple little exercise create these statements?"

The bubbles over the cartoon characters are similar to bubbles you may be carrying over your head you do not realize others are able to understand, even if they can not clearly state it. Think about someone you immediately had this weird feeling that something is not right, and you walked away from the experience thinking there is more to their story. How many others have experienced that with you?

Remember, the layers you are beginning to reveal are more obvious than you realize to everyone around you without you being aware of the impact of the message and presence you are exuding. This exercise is able to be repeated as often as you like and with as many as you like. Although this exercise

creates different results, it always creates awareness that the individual did not have before they completed the exercise. Feel free to share as long as you let them know where they can find more information, or have us walk a whole group through this with a coach facilitating the discovery and what is next.

Let me share more about each layer.

EXPLAINING THE LAYERS

As we mentioned in the introduction, ideally you have completed the exercises to create a starting point of discovery. It is completely okay if you feel like you did not understand the whole process. This is exactly why you are reading and going through the process. Now as we move forward to understanding the layers that make up all of you, you will create your own clarity in the process. Let me first share how I discovered this process.

HISTORY OF THE WHOLE EXPERIENCE

The whole process had other words to it when I was first discovering the journey. The World had an environment, beliefs, and engagement. History had conditioning, mind, and triggers. Organization had business, life wheels, and determination. Love had mind, body, and spirit. The experience had value, purpose, conversion, and embodiment. These words alone for each layer have so much depth. The words on the outside of the circle were merged to keep me seeking how to integrate them all with the BRAVE and WHOLE ladders in its own quadrant. All of our minds can get complicated,

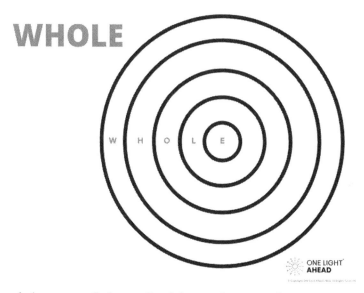

WHOLE

W H O L E

ONE LIGHT
AHEAD

and the reason I share all of this with you is that removing all these words didn't take any value away from the exercises or the experience. I keep the visuals and the memory to help us both see we all get to peel away layers that need some simplicity or perspectives.

As I was writing many papers for my Masters degree in Leadership I discovered many valuable quotes and reference materials such as this one in the the book, *Leadership on the Line.*

"Leadership addresses emotional as well as conceptual work. When you lead people through difficult change, you take them on an emotional roller coaster because you are asking them to relinquish something- a belief, a value, a behavior—they hold dear. People can only stand so much change at one time. You risk revolt, and your own survival, by trying to do too much too soon."

~Heifetz and Linsky, 2002, p. 117

This is true personally as well as professionally. Too often I have watched people resist looking in the mirror due to the fear of the unknown. The unknown causes lack of certainty. Yet, so often they do not realize the known is the opportunity to verify the evidence and value and be open to the unknown.

A very large percentage of people prefer to operate in the overall exterior world perspective. This seems comfortable. Yet, so many don't realize they have created a story for safety and in some cases some truly call it lazy. Those that desire to begin to be BRAVE and take the time—just like you are right now—discover after each experience and exercise that comfortable may not always be so comfortable. A coach shared with me years ago a story I will paraphrase for this false sense of security and comfort zone. He shared, "Many are preparing to die, and if that is the case, just bring in a casket and ask them to get in." It made me realize how realistic this truly is and how many may benefit from such a visual wake up call.

Looking inside, digging deeper, and unpeeling the layers has its challenges. Matthew West has a beautiful song about deciding to do more than just go through the motions. I don't know about you, yet I have had my moments of getting by, surviving, and telling myself I can make it to this milestone, or that one, only to discover the milestone came and passed and the BRAVE person I wanted to be was still buried in layers. This is why it is so important to me to share how these words and processes began before we dig into the BRAVE experience and exercise.

WORLD AS THE W IN THE WHOLE

Starting with the WHOLE experience and exercise, we know

the W represents the World, because it is the world we live in in it's unique state of communication. In this unique human experience we get to experience life in human form. The day to day, hour by hour and minute by minute moments have so much impact, much more than you would realize at first glance for some. The expectations, reactions, and impact it has is what we will discuss at much more depth. When the pandemic moved us to all virtual, audio, and visual communication processes we truly did change the makeup of our daily experience.

What do I mean? Some of us were born before Facetime, Tik-Tok, and all the other digital formats available today. I personally was exposed to Pac-Man, Texas Instruments, and had a phone on the wall. We had a very long cord to move around the house. These tools added lots of opportunities for different versions of communication. It also, in some cases, causes a false reality of what is true in day to day life. Every new digital form of communication leaves out so many details and distracts from unique connections.

Let me give you a silly example. Years ago, standing in the grocery store—in which there was a human clerk serving each and every person moving through the line—I noticed an interesting collection of items for the soul in front of me. Being the fun conversation starter I am, I said "So, that is a great group of items. What will you be creating with that collection?" I always enjoy the different responses and reactions I get from being such a jovial person. If I was buried in my phone or any other type of device or distraction, I may not have noticed or even created the communication. I started with a simple worldly observation, being curious, and asking a question—a simple concept.

The questions gave me the opportunity to learn more about

this person. The discussion developed into the next layer of our occupations and history. Had I not been willing to meet him in his world, I would have not discovered he was a local real estate company owner. We exchanged tangible business cards, and I got the opportunity to connect with him in the future. You will see I followed my own process to open the door, asking questions—using my chisel or slaying knife—and working through the layers as he invited me to open the doors.

The worldly external and internal perspective is the mask we all wear invisibly it may seem at some point and time. Some have learned how to live from the inside out and let all the layers be represented in our external experiences. Choosing to be transparent, vulnerable, and approachable in an extremely surface layer world is dangerous but deeply rewarding when you learn the process and the gifts of doing so. A 2008 movie called *Vantage Point* shares a visual recollection of eight strangers who are all witnesses to the same event. I would assign this movie (for those I knew it would give value) as a coaching assignment to help people see how to value multiple perspectives. We all experience our world from our vantage point and have opportunities to see others, if we choose.

HISTORY AS THE H IN THE WHOLE

History equals the H of the Whole which also has another layer of impact. As we discussed, the layers of the person are quite expansive and we get to address this in three ways. We get to address the family and environment, on to the habits and examples of how this shows up for some individuals as shared in the grocery store example. Every person is uniquely individual. Yet, one of my coaches told me after you have 10 years under your belt you will see some common patterns, and he was not joking. Another one of my coaches shared with me in every profession you go through maturity stages.

The maturity of history is also deeply related to perceptions, especially in family and environments. How often does a family member share a story they perceived one way and another swears that is so far from the truth in their mind? It happens in most every family and in every environment. Traveling to a multitude of offices and states, and working with team members in other countries, it is obvious how easily history may be perceived differently. The first writing coach I hired was from Australia. She heard just a few of my stories and said, "Well, at least you didn't end up as trailer trash."

A few years back I was in a Rotary meeting for a Granite Bay chapter. Those who don't know where Granite Bay is, picture your elite city and community in your neck of the woods. In Sacramento and Placer Counties of California, Granite Bay was considered one of the elite communities. At the meeting a sweet man was sharing how their group helped sponsor a church activity, and they granted all the kids that lived in the trailer communities of this area the gift to go. I then explained to him, I was one of those kind souls living in one of those trailer communities. At the time, I chose to invest in my business, so I rented a 700 square foot trailer to live in when I was actually in town. It made the man stop in his tracks and possibly realize everyone has their own stories and experiences.

Too often, people assume and create their own labels from their perception of history and worldly expectations. My boss when I was a high school Regional Occupation teacher said the same thing to me. Yes, I also taught high school and got a designated subject credential in less than two weeks, which is also unheard of in California. The story I told my boss was about how my roommate and my boyfriend at the time sold drugs from our apartment in Rancho Cordova. People are shocked to hear me share that at one short time, I was obsessed with what they called *crank* on the street. I thought I could solve the world in a few little white lines.

This was so not true, and when I came down (slang at the time for the drug wearing off) it was not pretty. My tips were stolen by my roommates to buy the drugs, and it took two traumatic incidents to get me to move out and stop. The first one was my boyfriend at the time holding me up against a wall with the iron I was using to iron my work shirt threatening me—if I asked another question he would hurt me. I shut up instantly. The second incident took much longer to heal from. I woke up with him sitting on top of me and his hands wrapped around my neck, our roommate at the door with his gun reacting to my screaming, and wondering why I couldn't breathe. This was all at the young age of nineteen.

Although there are many other stories I could share as we discuss each of our histories, I always believe that our own personal stories are the testimonies of survival and empathy to help others. These created our filters we see each experience through. Often when I choose my word for history it is complex. I have so much history it would take up volumes of chapters.

The one thing I have in my heart to share is why this book, *Slaying the Onion,* is so important to me. It took me many years to work through a few layers and then discover how many other onions this experience impacted others. I got to realize how the memories, perceptions, and challenges impacted myself, yet it also made me able to feel, empathize, and reframe the story to understand why many need to hear, see, or remember the story differently. Some even choose not to remember. I have a few of those myself as well. Many choose to sweep stories like the one I am going to share with you under the rug as it seems easier. My children will have their stories to tell, and I gave them plenty of ammunition to share as I was literally growing up with them as I got the gift to be their Mom.

I, just like my Mom, had our reasons and justifications for our good and poor choices. Thankfully, my Mom and I are respectful and compassionate most of the time, because we chose to keep our relationship in the midst of discussions we choose to not engage in due to lack of vantage points. I have learned to love and honor her to the best of my ability as my Mom. I hope this story gives other families the ability to learn to forgive and determine what they can and can not endure.

Of course, for me, I have also openly told my Mom there are some things she is no longer able to have trust in, and even my children may have that belief at times because we all make mistakes. We do not get to change the past, the choices we make, and/or the people. Every choice has a domino effect. This is only my perception of the journey I went through, and understandably I am aware everyone else has their perspectives. How we store and file away our story is how it affects our layers.

I was nine years old when my grandfather died. My grandfather's son, who was a half-brother to my Mom, came to visit for the funeral. My Mom decided we needed to visit them more often within a year or so after my grandfather's death. I still do not remember how many adopted children they had plus the six birth children I got to spend time with. We got to swim and visit lots of family in Palmdale, Califonia. Although I would often get pushed under water by the large six foot tall cousins on a regular basis, and there were many BBQs, it seemed like a great addition to our deeply caged lifestyle.

Many visits were enjoyable, fun, and helped us learn how much family we had. I do not remember the exact date and time when these visits ended. What I do remember is we would play the radio in my cousins' room and eventually it was to drown out the arguments between my Mom, my uncle, and his wife. I was about fifteen years old when I realized my Mom was locking her bedroom door and sharing a bed with my married uncle on numerous weekends for years. The explanation they gave my twin and me was that my Grandma lived with us, and the bedroom gave them a quiet place.

I ran away from home one day realizing that the choices my mom was making were not normal in any world. I ran all the way across the street to a kind neighbor. My mom came and dragged me out and slapped me across the face when I accused her of inappropriate behavior. In my silly memory, she told me it was none of my business.

My dear neighbor gave me a tape I still have today by Twila Paris, who I got to hear in concert many years later. My favorite song was "Warrior is a Child." This tape was my saving grace through getting old enough to move out, raising children, and so much more. I got punched one more time by my twin when he was running away from home for many of the same reasons. I was in his way and got the wrath of his anger. Our uncle justified his presence as our so-called father figure. The breaking point was when my twin told him he was not our father and no longer had a voice in his life. I do remember all of the cousins meeting one day knowing what was happening, sharing how we knew it was extremely unhealthy and if there was anything any of us could do.

Now, years later, a few of these cousins have chosen to be connected to myself and my Mom. One I was completely surprised by and the other never mentioned any of the memories in our conversation, and I did not feel it was my place to address any of the perceptions they have. I do believe that meeting was part of what stopped our visits. Sadly, It did not stop his visits to our home. I heard years later that his wife never chose to divorce him for the benefit of the children. I share this story not to hurt anyone, as I am positive if my children decide to write a book one day they will share the awful ways they remember how I impacted their lives—if I don't share it first in a future book.

The whole situation among many other dominoes created my understanding of family roles and I had no voice to make any impact at the time. Fast forward years later and I ended up working in Palmdale, Californai, as a coach. I was a productivity coach during the day with 85 people on my coaching roster, and lenders were on my evening roster for my own coaching business, One Light Ahead.

Thankfully, with the help of some powerful leaders, exposure to Love Languages, Fierce Conversations, and 21 Laws of Leadership, and so many more, I got to see how the historical experiences including being abandoned by my biological dad at five years old was impacting how I was showing up as a coach. A coaching client actually got upset with me once saying I did not share enough about myself. I thought then that people did not hire me to know about me. What I have learned, coach, and train is I get to walk people inside themselves, inside others, and inside of me as they are ready so we may gain true *agape* intimacy with ourselves and others. *Agape*—another term for unconditional love and intimacy— is the ability to truly know yourself and others. Although intimacy can be seen in other perspectives, it is truly an art for any relationship, especially the one you have with yourself.

I got to hear many stories since then from my biological father, from uncles and aunts, and even one from my other uncle who married my Mom when her sister (that he was married to) died. Without exposing too many details, understanding all of this story is my history and I did not ask permission from my Mom or anyone else impacted by this story—it is mine to tell how I experienced it in my life. The uncles ended up talking to each other and discussing my Mom and her choices. I also had two ex-husbands meet to discuss what they felt was wrong with me. I'm sure that impacted my children as well.

I am sure not everyone makes the poor choices some of us have made believing we filled some need or want. My kids and I both paid a price as many other children do. I watched a family at a gas stop and saw the children being impacted by their Mom and thought how many of us have unhealed hurts that impacted others. "My filters have filters," is what my last ex-husband said.

I have taken years in counseling working with multiple coaches, and what I have found over and over again—my stories give me empathy and compassion for others. I also know the value of grace and mercy. I get to be a clean slate and vessel every day from the redemption I gladly receive moment by moment.

"Habits, values, and attitudes, even dysfunctional ones, are part of one's identity. To change the way people see and do things is to challenge how they define themselves."
~Heifetz, Linsky, 2002, p.37

As you read my story and many others as we move forward, understand we all give ourselves our own identity with our memories. We get to choose to see if there is true evidence and value in keeping these identities. My Mom made choices that caused many identity concerns for many. Finally, the day I was giving a Becoming Brave women's retreat with a dear friend and some amazing women, it struck me—somehow I saw how many others were impacted in those experiences. It was then I realized I had removed the identity of the victim in this experience and so many other situations. I have been removing shackles of fear, obligation, and so much more over the years as I get to liberate others as well.

Recently I saw the same revelation as I was liberating someone from an identity of scarcity and survival. A coach asked me recently, "When will you see the stairs to your new stage?" I saw it the minute I showed my clients the stairs to their new stage or identity as we are discussing it here.

"Unintentionally and unknowingly we fall back into our imperfections. Bad habits are like living roots that return. These roots must be dug away and cleared from the garden of our soul."
~Scazzero, p.21

Cleaning out, reframing, and clarifying evidence is how I get to learn my history, adapt, and create the history I want to experience for myself and others. Take time to dig and clear your garden.

ORGANIZATION AS THE O IN THE WHOLE

How do we organize our schedule? Our clutter/space and how does this impact our leadership and life overall?

Day to day choices get organized by our willingness to be aware of how we choose. If security and safety are important to me, which it is to most, every choice may be organized by how safe does this make me feel? If your history is infused with abandonment and prison confinement concerns, then choices are organized around questions like, "How do I feel in control of my freedom, and how do I have space to roam while knowing where those I care about are located?" In my family we have an app called Life360, and even when we really don't want to talk to each other, we almost always know where each other physically is. Strange yet true.

Just recently I banged on my son's door, and he opened the door, frustrated with me. "What are you banging for?" Seeing his frustration, I said, "Well, if you wouldn't have pushed the SOS alarm to all of us, I would not have had to come to find out why." Thankfully, he said, "Oh," laughed, and commented on the joy of knowing the app worked to notify us all. Thankfully, it was a false alarm. I let him know another alarm gets a call to the police, false or not.

Sometimes the paths of our life journey take time. Let me share another client's story he was kind to share at an event years later. In my first few years of building One Light Ahead, I worked inside market centers, and in one center I had numerous clients. One of their vendors posted on Facebook they were looking for a coach. Many shared with this person they needed to talk to me. We got connected, and I coached this person for over a year in multiple areas.

Although she was at the top in her game personally, she asked if I would work with their husband. He ended up meeting with me after much resistance. To paraphrase, he said, 'I don't want more business, April. Although I know you may help me with that, I have been told you also have a spiritual focus, and I want to align in that more deeply.' After a little bit of getting to know each other, he finally started to be willing to complete each assignment I would give him. He came and spoke about the best assignment I gave him, which was to write his own eulogy. He said he often reflects on it since at the time the assignment was given he was in stage four cancer, and he truly did not know whether the next day was going to happen. He is in remission now, and his whole family has transformed from their commitments to look in the mirror, let someone inside their WHOLE lives, and help them reframe what they wanted to organize and why. Life is short, and how we organize each day, each choice, and every relationship is a daily experience. Determine today how you filter your organization process.

Love as the L in the WHOLE

What we love so impacts our layers. The passion and purpose we show up with and share is one phase of this powerful layer. The way we project it and give it currency is another discussion. It is extremely important to not jump layers. As we have seen moving from the world's exterior layer many will not want you to know anything about them. They prefer this comfortable and not so comfortable layer because removing the locked up layers requires work. They also discover there are layers to the layers.

I realized I had my layers in a maximum security prison. Anytime I thought *I let someone in*, as one of my coaches would say, I would remove layer upon layer until they hurt me, and then I would super glue them all back. Thus anyone getting through the numerous layers in my history and organization process I thought made some headway.

Yet after touring Brushy prison, a tourist location now of a prison that was open from 1896-1996, I got to personally experience what a maximum security cell looks and feels like. The layers that a human being went through to be in this location as a guard or as a prisoner were unexplainable in some respects. The maximum security prison many of us have actually hindered our journey, and in the next chapter we will dig deeper into this discovery.

Love has multiple perspectives. Intimacy is a trust journey where love may be established in a parent relationship, a partner relationship, or any relationship for that matter. The self love we also learn to experience gives us the ability to love others at a deeper level, because we have taken the time to dig through our own layers.

The final days I got to spend with my biological father helped me start addressing some of my locked layers. He sent me my first birthday card when I was 33, and I actually got the exact same card from my Mom that year. They hadn't talked in years. Although I saw him for a quick moment when I was 19, my half-brother called when our Dad was diagnosed with pancreatic cancer. We all gathered in August of 2016 where my twin got to verify he wouldn't hit our father. We ended up having a great visit in midst of all the history we all were working to process internally.

I almost closed my business during this time as I was working through my own realization there was no more time to address this relationship. It was now or never. A kind friend gave me some space to digest and reflect and thankfully some clients hung on with me while I closed our office. This is also when I found a deep appreciation for craft brews. I took time to read *Love Does* by Bob Goff and do some deep dives and finally went to visit him two more times. Instead of my father saying, "Thank you for coming," he said, "I knew you would come," on our one and only Thanksgiving dinner I remember. He cooked me breakfast, cranky through the process because he had stopped all radiation and was in hospice by then. I knew this would be our last visit, and most of it was sitting in the same space watching some type of television. I don't remember what was on the screen. My uncles and my cousin just sat with us. Strange how families communicate without communicating. That day opened the door for a deeper relationship with my St. Andre family. My uncles showed me a new style of love that day for their brother and this niece they didn't really know. For some reason, I felt the need to be in this space realizing this was enough to end this journey.

Thankfully, my uncles, cousins, and brothers get many other opportunities to make time for each other as we are able. There were many layers of world, history, and organizational perspectives to work through, that may or may not be worked through. Either way, we all value our intimacy across the miles we got to create in the unique path our lives have crossed.

Love is a process for families, for couples, and for companies. Today, I listened to a speaker share how he learned how to create intimacy for his teams. He chose to deeply love each person he got to spend time with, because that is what caused him to earn and value trust with them and for them. The books he mentioned were *The Trusted Advisor* and *The Trust Equation*. Intimacy is part of this equation. I too had an equation when I started as a coach about behavior. I learned it from a coaching-based-on-behavior book I once read. The equation was:

Abilities equals Performance plus what you are told or taught multiplied by motivation, divided by external sources equals results.

A simpler form of this equation is an event plus a reaction or response equals the outcome. One of my wise leaders in Palmdale taught me to take my complex and simplify. One of my current coaches shares in his book *The Truth About Stress* his own equation: Event to Belief to Choice will either create a positive or negative result. (Flint, p. 19) Love is an event, and how we respond or react to it equals our outcomes.

Agape Love as defined by Dave Blanchard in the book, *Today I Begin a New Life*, is "a heightned level of awareness.'"

"Agape Love requires that we climb up and out of our personal agenda and baggage—our unhealthy habits of thinking—and see the bigger picture."

Trust and intimacy are absolutely part of the equation as well. This agape love layer has many layers and taking the time to understand, value, and share the depth is valuable.

EXPERIENCE AS THE E IN THE WHOLE

Our presence, both visual, physical and perceived, is the layer that determines our connections. We will complete out the external and internal perceptions in this core of your WHOLE. Our core is the area aching to get released. I have asked many what life would look like to you when you no longer needed or chose to have walls. The answers are relatively similar—"I could not imagine that even though I think of it often."

To get to our core layers someone has earned the gift to connect, confirm, and clarify our deepest values. They have identified with and resonate with them in some form or fashion. They have created a form of intimacy. In most communication circles, these are limited to five people. This is why you learn to pay attention to the five people around you that are not your relatives. These are people you surround yourself with daily, weekly, or monthly, or in some cases as time or space will allow.

Take a minute to think about how they love, work, and what values they have. This will tell you a great deal about your inner circle. How many of these people have earned the space to know what you love? How do you share it with them? These are the experiences that show in your inner core experiences. We will talk more about these inner core experiences in the BRAVE exercise.

As I am writing these words I am enjoying a beautiful lake view in Zephyr Presbyterian Center. My amazing friend and I decided last year we were going to make an annual visit to this sacred place to share time to write, connect, and recharge. We know each other so deeply we know how and when to speak, how to support each other in our writing and in our recharge time. This is because we have taken years to work through each other's layers.

We were walking up a large flight of stairs. I climbed 11 times up the stairs to beat her by one this trip—we have a small competitive side. My fitbit told me I did 150 flights of stairs that weekend to give you the endurance required. It was obvious to me she had something troubling her and I patiently waited for her to share.

She does the same for me. She is able to make one statement with such tonality. I know how much more she is saying without her expressing one word. It will usually take me 20 minutes or so later in our conversation for me to acknowledge her point. Of course, she knew I would. This is from years of us knowing each other and what we experience in our worlds. We have taken time to know what has caused our triggers, know our communication styles, when and how we choose to organize our process, who and how we love, so that we truly show up experiencing each other as the best of friends we are. This did not happen overnight. We both went through phases of understanding and valuing each other through the invitations we gave each other into our layers. This is just one of my deeply connected experiences and friends who share these experiences with me.

Another friend I get to see less often and have known for less time still has a depth of connection and understanding. We both also invited each other into our layers one conversation at a time. She recently visited me in Tennessee after she and her husband went to see my ex-husband, which is how I met them. She then went on to share a Facebook feed of our pictures in the same feed. She had mentioned when we met that my ex was dating and then shared the picture on Facebook.

I am sure she didn't even consider how it would come across to me, and because we have such a valuable experience I took time to share on a *Possibility Monday* video which can be found on our *One Light Ahead* page the first public announcement of my divorce, because I realized I am happy for him. She gave me the opportunity to be publicly and privately aware I was liberated from the process, and it is okay to share it. It is friends who know you deeply enough to know when it is okay to nudge you without either of you deeply discussing it.

One of my friends was brave enough to walk Brushy prison and walk inside a Tennessee labyrinth with me. They help me see perspectives I would not have seen without them. They are a friend I am working to nudge as they are working to nudge me in our unique ways of life. We have learned how to appreciate our differences and how to clarify when and how we may spend time together. Ironically, their father worked as a prison guard, which gave me insight that any normal visitor would not have.

A friend years ago told me, you do not let a whole lot of people get too close to you. He was right and although we worked together, his wife and family were part of the church I attended at the time, I was still very new in the onion layer slaying process. I was just beginning to learn what it meant to experience the layers and let others walk inside mine. I have since connected with a multitude of friends I could mention as my other five friends, and all of them have a special place in my heart. The two I want to share with you are the ones that have caused me the most growth recently.

One I have known for years from afar through a leadership conference. They were kind enough to be a vessel for me over the years. They helped me discover what adventure looked like and how to decide what I want my future adventures to look like. I gather seashells now from each beach I get to visit moving forward. They also helped me understand that wishful thinking is no longer a wise place to live. I was always a silly fairytale girl who thought if she did enough, gave enough, or *anything* enough, everything would work out the way I planned. Silly belief system it was. I have since realized I get to choose the key people I surround myself with from real evidence, real facts, and tangible layers we invite others into in all respects of our lives.

Finally, the fifth and realistically most important person I have learned to give the biggest space to is me, myself, and I—along with the Holy Spirit living within. So many may relate with what I am going to say next. I used to be the last person on my list. I gave so many, and I paid the price.

It was a wise friend who asked me, "What do you want?" At that moment, the visual I saw was the chains were gone. Like the elephant I get to discuss weekly on my podcast, *my elephant and shackles were gone.* I was no longer living in the obligation cycle I had created, and I was ready to step into the light of my own being. Yes, BEING! You will get to learn more about that as we get to BRAVE.

Summary

All of our walls, layers, and stories are chapters to self-discover our highest potential, and we get to journal them if we choose. We get to discuss them with others. Join our community and start discovering together. You get to choose who and how you invite anyone into your layer without judgement. No one decides for you when you choose *you*!

Take the time to understand these walls and jail cells are all locked by *you*. Your fear is keeping you locked inside and *you* have the key. Learning to trust yourself and who you choose to surround yourself with is the next discerning choice we all get to make. Choosing to see who is toxic in your life— including if you are in victim mode, then you are toxic to yourself. Remember every choice is attached to a layer, and that has another layer in most cases. Let's walk deeply into these jail cells before we take on the BRAVE approach.

Living Unlayered Chapter Two Commitments

- I choose to meet people at the layer we are both aligned to meet at!
- I choose to invite safe agape love individuals into one layer at a time!
- I choose to reveal layers slowly with discernment!
- I choose to understand that my history has multiple perspectives!
- I choose to organize my slaying by asking questions surrounding my history!
- I choose to love others from agape love, sometimes from a distance!
- I choose to experience myself and others as a living unlayered intimate soul!

CHAPTER THREE

Jail Cells to the Layers

"If we wish to free ourselves from enslavement, we must choose freedom and the responsibility this entails."
~Leo Buscaglia

The more I share the process and inspire others to walk through one layer at a time, I see the jail cells we have kept ourselves in. I realized just recently my WHOLE self was in maximum lockdown so afraid of letting anyone see all of me. The vulnerability of opening one door after another is so extremely scary. Realistically in the world we live in, we do get to be choosy about how we give permission to truly know us and how they get to know us. Yet, the most important one you want to know every bit of you is YOU! Again, that lack of being willing to see yourself in the mirror and love the person you are in all the depths of layers is what brought you to today.

One of my coaches actually said to me the other day, take time to look in the mirror and see the wonderful lady you are. Just hearing this made me emotional to realize the truth to the statement and how difficult this is to do for many just like me. I am wonderful! I am beautifully made and my scars, stories, and stepping stones all were part of the journey. Yet, they also kept me trapped in guilt, fear, and shame for way too long. Let me say more about my own experience with these jail cells to help you understand how I know how to see it in others.

At an early age my Mom was deeply afraid of her children getting hurt. My brother and I are twins and we had a crib, playpen and then a gate that kept us in the room of my Mom's choice until we could climb over it. I remember our puppy was given freedom and we got to pet him from inside our first jail cell. She then decided we needed a door locked from the outside that she sawed in half so she could see in, yet we could not see out. We were then in our new jail cell, the "playroom" she called it. The four foot front yard and six foot backyard fence was the next phase when we were allowed outside. These were tangible memories of real jail cells for me personally because they created real prisons in my mind, heart, and soul.

Thankfully I had many mentors, and one I even called my adopted Dad—ironically a retired police officer—who started guiding me to Freedom, giving me opportunities to experience life through putting me on stages for speaking, peer counseling, and so much more.

As I go on to share more about my own experiences, I know that each of our experiences not only cause a lock on our heart, mind, and soul, they sometimes create a multitude of locks that domino and trigger each other by security systems we didn't even know existed. Yet, we all have the keys if we are willing to choose to open the locks and the emotions or stories attached to them. As I walk you through a few of my own and a few of my clients with their permission, we will discover together freedom is way more liberating than the locked down prison we allow for one too many years.

Let's discuss Hazel's story first from her words.

"I feel like I've always known I have walls. Seemingly walls to protect me, but through this journey—I'm aware that some walls have been erected to hurt others. Sorta the same thing, but actually not even close. As we came to a close on our time working as a group, but only slightly moving the earth of what will be a continued journey, the notion that my walls are interconnected and form a castle around me truly took shape. April called it a castle for a while and I imagined a pretty medieval castle, like any princess could be worthy of, and while knowing it kept me shut away from others, myself, and truly living life—it looked pretty. Pretty is one more "hook" to keep one from moving things too much. It infers investment in the space and a comfortability there. What's weird is my castle only has small windows, apparently no roof because I always envisioned getting a ladder tall enough to look over the top better at the world around me, and only one behemoth wood door.

As we closed our session, we discussed the tethers keeping our hot air balloon of the life I am able to live tied to the ground. One immediately left to mind. Then my mind said how do you attack that tether? You better find one that you can think more clearly (read: easily) through. Well—so now I "must" choose this tether, because my resistance was so immediate! So, I chose to attack Shame.

How does one attack a tether, and what in the world connects it to the castle? Well, for me they were one in the same. You can't live the life you are able to, of freedom, if the balloon is tethered. You can't live the life you are able to, of freedom, if you are inside a castle with tiny windows, and a door so big you are unable to move it. Now I'm not imagining the other rooms in my castle, I'm only seeing four solid walls (with a tiny window or two), like a turret that I'm trapped in with walls of shame surrounding me and boxing me in because they are so high up. So, I can't reach the top to try to take one of the stones/rocks away from the wall in a neat and orderly fashion, it's going to be messy. Okay, so I can only focus on the rocks that form the edge of the tiny window.

I grab a tool (some sort of study stick in my imagination) and start working to remove the grout surrounding one of the rocks. It's a workout for sure, and I believe the only way to attempt to ensure the rock doesn't find it's way back to it's former spot is to recite Bible verses of Truth over it. I recite the first Bible verse that comes to mind to counteract the shame I feel about the memory associated with why this rock was placed here in the first place.

> *"Therefore, there is now no condemnation for the those who are in Christ Jesus, because through Christ Jesus the law of the Spirit who gives life has set your free from the law of sin and death."*
>
> ~Romans 8:1 NIV

I'm crying, both from the exertion to loosen the rock, but also because I long to believe God's word over me and actively need to work to not rebuff it as not for me. This is no easy task, and the repetitive quoting of scripture seems to seep into me more each time I say it. I'm not angrily quoting it at myself, like I should know better. I'm not crying, because it's so hard to believe.

But as I work on the rock, I find that I grew stronger in the connection of God's love for me, His precious daughter who has walled herself away from Him too, and knows this is the right hard thing to be focused on. Finally, the rock comes loose. But now what? I'm standing in the middle of a round room that has no door, and knowing that I want to, get to, choose to, remove another rock in the wall. I only have two hands, what to do with the rock. Glancing around, I notice the floor isn't really a floor but rather just dirt. I don't want to place this rock too close to the base of the wall, because that seems like "reinforcing" whatever those bedrock stones of the wall are. Why reinforce it accidentally now, but rather how do I be intentional about what to do with this rock. How can I use all the things this rock is for positive. This rock has history, a story to it, and it relates to shame that I felt over an instance/interaction/etc; but it also has a new memory associated with it of this Truth from God. The imagery is that both the shame and the scripture are now engraved in the rock, and you can see it on the surface.

What to do? That's when it hits me. Images of gardens that have blooms, growth, and aliveness in them. And the paths that can guide you through the aliveness that is the garden. Aha! That's what these stones can be—the path through the garden that is and will be my life as it can and will be in freedom!

Now there is the process of digging a hold with my little tool, so that I can place the rock in the ground to start a path. Once that is secure, I turn and look to the next rock in the wall to attack. Rinse and repeat. Soon, I will have a larger window or new door to move in and out of; but not to run away through. Likely it will open up more space so that the path being built will meander and wind through the lands, but I will continue to come back until the walls are down and placed as a path through my life of freedom. And while maybe a bit overwhelming to think of the big picture, of all the paths to be built out of a castle of may walls (need to impress, need to pretend, fear, shame, and perhaps others), I can do it. I know this because I just did one rock, with one verse of God's Truth. I have many more resources available to me as I work to chip away at what once protected me, but now feels stifling."

Hazel's story reminds me of the scripture:

> *Praise be to the God and Father of our Lord Jesus Christ, the Father of compassion and the God of all comfort, who comforts us in all our troubles, so that we can comfort those in any trouble with the comfort we ourselves receive from God.*
> ~2 Cor. 1:3-4

This was the first scripture that ever got written on my heart. Some reading may not immediately resonate with me or Hazel's reference to scripture, yet the layers and journey we all have been on are very much real. May you go into each next jail cell reference or wall contemplating how they relate with your own and what you need to unlock your own.

Hazel spends an immense amount of time in imagery and analysis paralysis. Sometimes she will confess to avoid the action she knows she needs to take and taking one rock at a time is her own jail cell of analysis. I related with her castle as I stepped into Brushy prison on June 26th of 2021. Relief is what we both felt as we literally walked outside the prison gates. A real tangible physical sigh of relief. My friend literally said he remembered at that moment what he felt when he knew he was saved.

This, for Christian friends, is the moment you choose to surrender your life to Christ. I knew before we even got to the location stepping inside the physical walls of a maximum security prison was going to be difficult to express. The deeper we walked in, one gate after another, one building after another, the depth of fear, anxiety, emptiness, and darkness was extremely overwhelming. Every stomach muscle clenched, my chest was heavy, and my heart ached for the pain these prison walls echoed. The pain of the prison guards and the families they all impacted.

This pain is deeply real for everyday citizens who have the ability to roam free in our world and instead choose their own maximum security lock down. We all lock ourselves in and wonder why we feel isolated, abandoned, and depressed? Have you had any of these challenges? There are days even when you think you have unlocked the prison and you find yourself back inside the walls of the cell. It has taken me years of counseling, coaching, and relentless self discovery including walking these walls to know how to express the depth of pain I felt inside these walls.

All the pain you may feel when you recall your history discovery, the way we organize our thoughts and experiences, as well as how we love all come from the jail cells we have or have not created. The challenge is we may tell our brain we love safety and security because our history shows us evidence of what previous pain looks like. We end up keeping the cell locked to stay in this pain. Or as I learned as we walked the numerous jail cells, we throw our crap on the guards walking by our life.

This shocked me as I learned that this is a very normal occasion in prisons and in military situations for prisoners to throw urine and feces on the passing by guards. Yet, I

saw the realization in how each of us throw our victim crap (garbage stories as real or as self created as they are) on the ones who we thought were supposed to protect us, who we thought could have done something so we couldn't get hurt and then wonder why they are emotionally, intimately, physically, or spiritually guarded with us. Some of these may have deserved or still deserve the crap thrown on them, yet reliving the story over and over again just causes pain.

When my son was kidnapped because I hired him to work an event with me. I knew he was tired and I let him borrow my truck to go see a friend. I forgot to get gas before I gave it to him. He stopped to get gas and took a few minutes to close his eyes. He didn't realize he had not locked the doors and two men kidnapped him, one in the truck and one behind him. One has already been convicted and the other one is in process, thus the rest of the story goes into that journey. Thankfully, he never threw any crap at me, yet I did enough of it for him. It took a client when I was sharing the story to remind me how sad it was for the attackers to feel the need to do something like they did. I had not even taken time to consider their perspectives, their jails, or stories that caused them to act in such a way. My son has to experience the domino of their decisions for the rest of his life and still gave the kindness of his heart to let the first one create a plea deal. My own self-berating took a while to let go of and release my own disappointment in myself for the contribution I had in this story. It was quite a cell for a while and I am thankful I raised some extremely resilient people in midst of my own challenges. They would tell you I helped create their resilience and they would be accurate.

The even more exciting other side of the coin is the opposite benefit of crap! As I was sitting in one of my coaches final 30 year event we ended up discussing crap. A man I just got through golfing with the previous day shared that he had multiple football fields of crap that was now a profit center for him. He has learned that he can use it to fertilize the thousands of acres of crops he has. Yes, the same crap we have thrown can now be fertilizer?

This is the gift of reframing and understanding that in order to open the door to your jail cell, you get to reframe the experience and make it fertilizer! Just like the sad situation my son had to go through and many others my children have overcome, we are all learning how to make them fertilizer. I also learned that I am unable to decide the time frame they need to work at. It is their journey to walk and I will be the one taking the crap they want to throw until they are ready to make fertilizer. Any person being the receiver of this crap throwing understands this pain and chooses to set healthy boundaries for the journey.

You probably have situations like that where you may see how someone else is throwing crap and you may not even see how you are doing the same to someone else. I know I have done it. When my daughter decided to stop talking to me from what I believe is a deep misunderstanding, I remembered when I did not talk to my Mom for years and decided to give her space to work through her belief. I made a small mistake in words and choices that I am sure I will pay for in years to come, which was another reminder of how to step out of the cell. We all make them. How we choose to respond to them is our choice. I am choosing to not let her put me in a jail cell and I am letting her decisions and reactions determine when she is ready to see the fertilizer opportunity. I take the responsibility I have and let others take theirs. Not easy when you talk about family relationships or any kind for that matter. We all have triggers, emotions, and history we are working through. My choice caused all of her other triggers from mine and others previous poor choices to come up, and she decided I was a great target for her pain. I am choosing to be her prison guard from a distance.

Thankfully, I know she is a smart, loving, and capable woman who will overcome in her way and in her time. I know our relationship eventually will be mended in some form or fashion and even if it was just to write this awareness, it will serve its purpose.

Remember, for all of us who have made mistakes and put ourselves in jail cells, as well as given permission for others to throw crap on us, there is another perspective. This crap has great potential to be fertilizer!

MAKING CRAP FERTILIZER

Years ago I was exposed to the concept of moving from point A to point B. The visual graphic will help give some ways of seeing the journey.

Over the years I have added my own perspectives including clarifying how to move crap to becoming fertilizer. Of course, there is a multtitude of ways to understand fertilizer as well.

As I will share in Chapter 6, my own crap became a wealth of mustard seeds. A *Sunset* article reminds us these nutrients help us create our growth and an expansive set of roots from fertilizers. "The nutrients help strengthen the new plants' developing stems and encourage the growth of a dense network of roots."

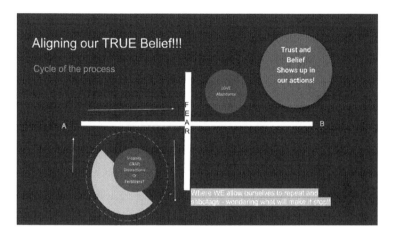

Adding to this research, we understand that we get to determine what part of each of the fertilizers are healthy for what we want to survive and thrive. An example including the previously referenced graph is when a client says to me they are stuck in point A when they believe with every ounce of their being they want to be at point B. Their desire to be at point B is what drives this verse Isaiah that says:

"Build up, build up, prepare the road!
Remove the obstacles out of the way of my people."

One of my clients who lets me share a great example of this crap to fertilizer is when they moved to a new city. In their mind they kept telling themselves they were new. This same client has sold over 700 homes so far in her career and finally realized in one of our FREE Q and A sessions you can register for at https://onelightahead.com/love-what-you-do-again/ she made the choice to move to add value to her life and she transformed the crap mindset into a fertilizer to enjoy reminding herself of her expertise, her joy of the business, and how much value she is now bringing to her new community.

Of course, this is a simple example of a relatively easy transformation of thought patterns. Ironically on another episode of Adddressing the Elephant in the Room Podcast you can listen to a coach openly see the mindset opportunity to transform and immediately put himself back in a jail cell by choice, Season 4 Episode 2.

Remember, each of us get to decide which part of the scarcity and crap side or Fertilizer—Abundance, Belief, Faith and Trust side. Which side do you want to truly align with?

SUMMARY

We get to discover the key to our jail cells. We get to invite others into our prisons and we get to decide when we don't want to live in a prison any longer. In our final chapter we will discuss what I believe is the ideal path to live in. It has some spiritual perspectives and a seed to consider if you are willing. The jail is one locked gate after another and the layers have their own challenges. When I walked into the Brushy, it was in the cafeteria I felt the deepest sadness. This location has this impact because just like in our day to day life, we go through our daily life necessities. Unlike for the prisoners, they had no other place to go and if they even attempted to step out of line, they could lose their life. If our survival depended on unlocking our jail cells and finding fertilizer opportunities, then would we be more urgent about the time and effort? It does, by the way!

Living Unlayered Chapter Three Commitments

- I realize some my own jail cells are of my own making!
- I realize I have the key for each layer and for each lock!
- I realize I get to choose when I am ready to open each door!
- I realize I am safe and capable of discerning the stories attached to each lock (and it is also completely acceptable to ask for guidance, help, and support in the journey)!
- I realize I am responsible to seek out tangible facts to support the truth in each story!
- I realize I get to create new stories and fertilizer to remove the jail cell!
- I realize I create my FREEDOM one story, one layer, and one unlocked cell at a time!

CHAPTER FOUR

LEARNING TO BE BRAVE

Be bold, be brave enough to be your true self.
~Queen Latifah

Y our choice to BE the person who chooses you, what matters to you and choose to share it with others is exactly what we wrote this book for. We know that just one life in every city, state and country will light this whole world and that started with you. Make sure to add your light to our map at www.onelightahead.com when you have completed the whole book.

BRAVE is represented by five letters and words as the WHOLE exercise was. The BRAVE concept has been used for years in so many formats. A friend of mine and myself actually created a whole womens' group about Brave Women Becoming. In the journey before then, I was realizing for myself how challenging it was to be BRAVE in my own vulnerability, my own challenges, and especially my own confidence. Although so many thought I was ridiculously confident. It has taken years to realize how BRAVE I have been, am today, and will be tomorrow. This is exactly what this concept is all about, learning the depths of the concept!

You are choosing to walk through the concepts of discovering from the inside out. This seems like a simple concept, and yet it is so not! I am living proof that most live on the outside reactive side. Many react to what the world tells them to react to as we discovered in the World exercise. In this exercise you are actually going to do the exercise after you complete the journaling and reading of each of the layers and sections of the BRAVE to get the depth of integrity you may not even know you are challenged to have with yourself.

My best friend, bridesmaid, editor—and so many other wonderful adjectives I give my dear gift of a leader and friend—had the most challenging moment doing this exercise when it hit her so hard how out of integrity she was with herself. This is the time to give yourself grace. Remember, this is just you and me here deciding to say life is so precious and it is time to dive deeper into these layers. As I was walking another wonderful friend and coach through another experience she also realized in a light bulb moment how valuable her own ability to see herself—her BRAVE WHOLE self—was. Being able to see herself accurately gave her the tools she had been missing to see and others more accurately.

Ironically, it was that day when my dear bridesmaid had her trigger moment. It was when we took some time to go to a labyrinth location I deeply appreciate in the hills of Auburn Califonia. The Alta Sierra Biblical Gardens has quite a story. The labyrinth is something I have visited for years and on this day the visual awareness of how difficult it is for so many people to be able to walk inside themselves and keep digging silently, prayfully, and precisely was so evident. The next enormous discovery came when I realized; not only do many not want to go this deep, they also do not know how to go this deep and then invite someone in to experience the journey with them. This was the first day I had shared the labyrinth with another person in such a way. I would go on to share it in an event with multiple people and hear amazing stories.

What does the labyrinth look like to you in your own discovery process moving forward? We get to circle the many walls of resistance you are experiencing to even get this far. I know all about what you are experiencing, as even in typing this message, I am forcing my tail to be in the seat and share these thoughts. It is difficult to realize that our own pain of not sharing is only hurting ourselves. It is the gift of being vulnerable, being genuine, and most importantly being able to forgive yourself is the pathway to inspiring another soul, just like I believe this journey will do for you.

Therefore, let us start the journey inside the core of who we are in our BRAVE self. We will add a little bit more explanation in advance before we start the experience.

B IN THE BRAVE EXPERIENCE™

B in the Brave stands for BE. When I would share this word with others in live presentations it was normal for people to have that expression of huh? What does BE mean? What does that mean to me? Who are you and what are you thinking? Yes, those expressions are quite humorous until they are not. It is challenging to understand the gift of just BEING. We are spiritual BEINGS having a human experience, in my humble opinion, and the BE of the process is how we show up.

How do we show up? Are we being completely present, completely engaged, and truly listening with complete commitment to be a gift to the person, situation, or experience? These are the questions among many others we are going to dive into as we keep discovering the depths of our internal life. Thank you for patiently reading, engaging, and deeply reflecting as this is no easy process.

BE, defined by the Webster's dictionary, means: a: *to equal in meaning and/or* b: *to have identity with*—which leads perfectly into the reality that identity and meaning are so deeply challenged in our daily world for almost everyone. The media icons of the world from Oprah to even Robin Williams—an amazing impactful soul when he was alive and even now—all struggled with this. Should we expect to be any different?

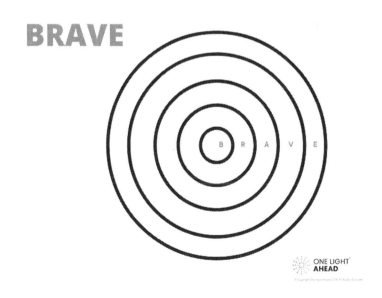

They publically shared their stories during or after the fact. Either way we all have some depth to cover.

BE is the deepest internal core of your values—who you identify and find meaning in. To some this would seem a relatively simple process to discover, and then, just as you think you know who you are, you realize there is another layer. A quote I was given years ago has an unknown author "Just when you thought you graduated from the school of hard knocks, they created another course." I am sure you may relate with this journey. Our layers are attached to these layers of hard knocks. Let's start the first step of your identification process through the layers you express who you are BEING.

Responsibility is the next layer that will help you discover your connections and who you are surrounding yourself with.

THE BRAVE EXERCISE™

As we discussed in the previous exercise, this also is about discovering your clarity into a multitude of layers, yet this one has an internal layer first and then an external layer. Remember to answer each specific question in less than a minute with your instantaneous response. This immediate response will discover far more than you realize and help the end product have more authenticity. There is no need to be polished or perfected in this exercise as it is just us.

Here we go:

How do I just BE?

Example for internal—I BE by being a vessel to each person, conversation, and experience for forward movement one light at a time.

External perspective—The BE the world I live in gets to appreciate is the authenticity I am constantly told I demonstrate.

YOUR TURN TO ANSWER THE FOLLOWING:

How do I just BE internally?
Who am I responsible for?
Who do I ATTRACT to my presence personally?
What value do I share from my internal VALUES and beliefs?
What experience do I provide to others that shares who I am choosing to be?
How do others perceive how I am BEING?
What external perspective represents this RESPONSIBILITY?
Who are the five people who externally represent the people I want to ATTRACT personally?
What values are consistent with the five people who are surrounding me consistently?
What experience do I provide to others that shares who I am choosing to be?
Who externally comments or praises about these experiences?

WRAPPING UP THE BRAVE EXPERIENCE

Now put them all together for the final tasks of this exercise:

As a value statement, even if you create a run on sentence, create a sentence with any of these words, phrases, etc that shares your BRAVE *internal* perspective.

By adding words or phrases, as many as you like, even if you create a run on sentence, create a sentence with these words about your *external* BRAVE perspective.

The Brave exercise is much deeper, and now you see why

we wait to dig into this one. The layers of integrity we have hidden, buried, and devalued is outrageous for most of us. We have a multitude of layers and reasons we do this. Yet, at the end of the day, your authentic BRAVE self is who you want to be sharing on a daily basis. This is where we start discussing the integration and bridging of these layers.

The bridge we will discuss in the next chapter is where you get to see for yourself and for others how easily it is to jump a layer before it is appropriate or timely. Og Mandino Leadership Institute—an organization I am thankful to be a certified coach with—teaches through habit finder materials that we naturally hold back 40 percent of our natural energy and cooperation. There are a multitude of resources I can share with those who want to know more about axiological mathematics, habits underneath the surface and how the day to day life experiences have created stories and sabotaging thoughts distracting your natural genius. The overall point is that as you keep reading, we will start the personalized process of helping you build more authentic relationships. You will learn more listening skills as you work through the layers of walls. Most importantly, You will learn more about how BRAVE you are in each path and conversation.

THE DEPTH OF BRAVE

As we did in the whole process, let's dig a little deeper into the BRAVE representations of the words and how they reveal the layers you truly want to reveal when you have found your fertilizer. Digging deeper into the words of each layer. Being who you choose and want to be is a daily commitment. As a previous client shared, choosing to write your own obituary and work backwards is a BRAVE visual experience. Every morning you wake up you get to reinforce the decision by what you say to yourself, what actions you choose to complete because of the thoughts you followed through with. We call this walking your talk. Onion Slayers slay each layer by living it out!

Every day I choose to be responsible for myself first, look in the mirror, and address all of my own elephants. I get to take one step closer to living completely from the inside out. Some may have seen the fabulous movie made by Pixar and Disney called *Inside Out*. I would tell people this is a great representation of what I get to do.

I resonated with the Joy character because this is who I deeply choose to be on a daily basis and let this emotion lead my thoughts as often as possible. Yet, just like the movie, I have had to learn how to look in the mirror to embrace sadness, disgust, anger, and fear as represented in the movie. They are scheduled to release eleven more emotions in the 2022 movie *Inside Out 2*. A speaker at the Global Leadership summit shared they hired skilled professionals to help them write, produce, and edit these characters. This movie is a great visual representation of how all the five emotions may be triggered.

Responsibility is the next layer that will help you discover your connections and who you are surrounding yourself with.

In the jail cells chapter we discussed our history impacts our emotions which impacts our thoughts to our actions. We get to choose responsibility, not to give it to others. When we find ourselves in Blame we fall short and get lost in victim mode. There is a time and place for real victim challenges as I shared in my son's story out of many others I could share.

Although Thursday evening, the night my son was kidnapped, was the worst night I could of imagined, until at 3:30 a.m. the coroner, who also served as sketch artist said, "Thankfully I am here as the sketch artist, not the coroner."

She reminded us in one sentence all we had to be thankful for. I told the three different law enforcement officers that called me that early morning, asking me if my son was sane, "I knew from my son's tone of voice he did not know if he was going to live another day. Please help us figure out what happened!"

Many parents have told me they don't know how they would of responded to such an incident.

Friday evening after our first day of the event we went on to be responsible for was done. It was my favorite part of the day to just watch my son sleep. Behind the scenes, even though we were not allowed to share anything of what happened, the police were doing their job. My truck was seized, and we went on about our weekend. I learned a great reminder in that moment to let go of anything that I no longer needed to be responsible for! Even my son said he didn't remember much of the event, and I have chosen to end these specific events to let go of this past and create a new fertile ground for Living Unlayered Events.

My daily responsibilities are to be responsible for who I am seeing in the mirror. Am I being who I am called to be? Am I showing up completely present? These are my highest desired opportunities of responsibility. Am I caring for the temple I am gifted with as I own my life wheel experiences. When I review my numbers in my life wheel are they aligned with the best self I may be? Do I surround myself with people who support, encourage, and empower the person I choose to BE?

Living from the inside out—being BRAVE is a step by step process. Living a life fully unlayered as you are ready to BE is a choice. I would not be fair to my ex-husbands, my children or family without owning my own lack of living unlayered numerous times. It is no accident my life is jam packed with stories because I allowed myself to surround myself with people who wanted to stay in the layer they were in with me. What usually ended each relationship is when I pushed for another layer and they wanted nothing more than what was. Every moment now, I choose to be constantly slaying each onion layer and inviting others into my life who desire to slay with me.

This is where I have constantly discovered I get to daily become the person I want to attract moving forward who desires to dig into deeper layers!

ATTRACTION OF THE BRAVE

This is where the attraction concept comes into play. When I see who I want to be, who I want to be responsible for, I get to pay attention to whom I want to attract. This is very important personally and professionally. Numerous authors will share their own perspectives. Our message, our presence, and our beliefs will attract the people we want or don't want into our lives. When we realize the people in our lives that are challenging are because you invited them in, this is where we get to decide what we want to be responsible for. A coach recently walked through the WHOLE and BRAVE exercise with me, and the light bulb moments happened for her. She shared the steps to the tools in this process that helped her realize who and what she was allowing in her life. She will be one of our coaches to the group programs we offer in the future. It gave her joy to see how BRAVE she was becoming.

Going back to the five people we are attracting. Recently I had a conversation with a coaching client, which I am positve will not be the first or last time.

I asked "When will you let go of being a doormat?' In my mind, every time I get to ask this question I reflect on a great movie created from a book written by Rene Gutteridge called *My Life as a Doormat* where the cast gets to address addressing conflict.

So many moments I too personally realized I had allowed myself to be a verbal, and at some cases physical, emotional, and spiritual punching bag for anyone who would show me attention.

At some points, including a rape that happened at the young age of 19, I had believed I deserved the beatings for a multitude of reasons. It has taken me years of coaching and counseling to reframe my own evidence.

This is why another client said to me, "It is obvious you have have taken your years of overcoming your own history to provide immense compassion and empathy."

Many clients hit a tender emotional moment when I get to be their mirror and remind them how valuable they are and how important their own beliefs move them forward. They all realize as they give me permission to be their mirror, I get the gift and invitation to work through their layers. The difficult part of all of our all belief systems is every one of them is attached to one or multiple layers. By learning to create new stories and unveil the potentials attached to the new stories is a journey, we get to discover what is attached to each story and layer.

Many hold on to these layers deeply, and it takes a deep commitment, decision, and release to choose to forgive yourself and others and determine what is a realistic new belief and identity.

This is not always an overnight process and requires belief, faith, trust and discovering new evidence, fact, and perceptions. Choosing to see, hear, and value yourself is a gift!

We get to make ourselves a priority and attract those who honor and value what aligns with what we say matters.

VALUE OF BRAVE

Value is a layer we get to meet people at. What value we share is another way we learn to connect and relate. We may hear, see, or determine something similiar quicky or it may take time.

Some may value sports, dance, the same authors, etc. Each layer of our values is sometime spoken and sometimes unspoken. Having an Abelson Disc Certification, I know that everyone makes a command decision mentally in seven seconds about a visual presence of another person, from what they are wearing, how they smell, and so many others perceptions. In every conversation there are three aspects to our communication.

Believe it or not, only seven percent of it is in the words we choose. The other major percentages depending on the statistics you subscribe to is tonality and body language!

Just like the bubbles over the cartoon characters we mentioned previously, how we show up sharing our value is perceived in a multitude of ways.

EXPERIENCE OF BRAVE

The ideal we experience we provide to others is when we live from the BRAVE internal core perspectives living completey unlayered. Our BEING showing up responsible, attracting those who share the same values or want to learn more about our values will be joyfully invited into another layer. A recent BRAVE experience I chose was to attend a Ballroom and Brews event. A dance instructor found a brewery to host a social outing.

They created a fabulous experience mixing two values and experiences to connect like minded individuals. To any of my AA or similar friends, finding an instructor of your similar values to create some socials such as hiking etc is another option.

The values our copywriter helped us discover was from a multitude of interviews she did with our clients and myself. Our website shares we are relentless—we are unapologetic about asking questions, and no surprise, we believe in Living Unlayered.

All would seem so obvious, yet they were not to me at the time. Often we think our values show up in our experiences. Our actions, beliefs, and choices are revealing more than we acknowledge often.

Clarifying, communicating, and committing to them from our Inside Out Internal BRAVE perspective is a beginning to choosing and owning what you say matters.

Living unlayered value for myself came from walking so many individuals, teams, and myself through digging into each layer. An example of this was the day I heard my copywriter used a fancy terminology, *icky*. It made me imagine what this meant for her. She uses this terminology often when something feels inauthentic or ingenuine, and it physically gets connected with an outward reaction every time she uses the terminology. She doesn't even realized we got it on video in a recent course she took with me. You can also hear her talk about how important these valuable experiences are on her podcast Season 4, Episode 4.

We all have these fun terminologies and visual physical reactions to something from our own triggers or experiences. So often when we get caught off guard by how we think we are experiencing a a relationship or being experienced in an event or process we may get stuck in our own bad habits, reactions, or external world perspectives. This is when we may choose to breathe, BE present, responsible attracting who we want to value this experience through and ideally create a whole new BRAVE experience.

SUMMARY

BRAVE experiences are created from choosing to BE in our gifting and presence celebrating who we instrincally are! It is our ultimate responsibility to attract and align with who and what we say matters!

Every day to day experience is impacted for all we cross paths with when we make these impactful choices.

Slaying your onion empowers you to take a look at all the layers of your life and who you are attracting, what you are attracting, and what is going on inside the process. Because you are this far in the process, you are obviously taking this seriously. Let me remind us both, we are imperfect. Nothing about this process needs to be perfect, and it is going to be a constant work in progress. Give yourself grace as you dig into each layer. Take time to reflect, discuss, and refine the journey along the way. Each of the exercises we have been doing will now take these reflections into how we build bridges moving forward in the next chapter.

LIVING UNLAYERED CHAPTER FOUR COMMITMENTS

- I choose to BE BRAVE!
- I choose to BE responsible for my choices!
- I choose to attract what I value and want to experience!
- I choose to live unlayered from the inside out!
- I choose to write my own eulogy or obituary to live it all out now!
- I choose to see and express my intrinsic value!
- I choose to experience BEING!

Chapter Five

Building Bridges—Relationship Value Exchanges

I like to see myself as a bridge builder, that is me building bridges between people, between races, between cultures, between politics, trying to find common ground.

~T.D. Jakes

Congratulations, you made it to the moment when you get to take all the work you have done looking within and understanding others and put it into action. Just like T D Jakes and others of us that feel called to build makeshift bridges to guide others to help build a sturdy or stronger bridge from the common ground, we get to build bridges in stages, understanding our own layers we are bringing to the process. We then get to connect the possible paths we are creating with the person you are attempting to connect with. Of course, this is also where you get to hear, see, and understand what they are bringing and how they will connect. More often or not, there are some simple layers to connect with and yet layer after layer there may be many more challenges. This is where we get to give and receive value!

As we discussed in the beginning of this book each layer

has many of its own walls. Each of us gets the opportunity to discover and empathize now we understand how our own layers have created so many of our own obstacles to build these bridges. It is so important to remember that as we build these bridges jumping paths, layers, or expectations may cause all the work you attempted to do to crumble. Take time to work through this process and make it worthwhile. There is a process and a reason for the process.

Often I have been told visuals and stories help others understand how best to relate. Therefore, each layer we will provide the visuals of the connections and then the final visual to the integrated bridges. The words may have seemed separate and unrelated as you worked through each layer, and yet once you see them all together, it will be amazing how it all unfolds. Year after year I share these bridges, and it still awes me how they unfold. This is actually the first time I get to walk you, my friend, through this part of the journey. Thank you for walking this far. It is such a joy to know there are individuals just like you that really want to live in a new world where we truly take time to learn ourselves and each other at a WHOLE new level and show up as who we are BRAVE to shine in and as. This journey is quite a process. So glad we get to walk it together.

World to Experience "WE" Bridge

The First connection may seem so appropriate and where the "BRAVE WHOLE WE" experience comes from. The Whole W represents the whole world and the E represents the BRAVE Experience word. The bridge shows a BRAVE individual living from the inside out meeting a WHOLE

Building the BRIDGE

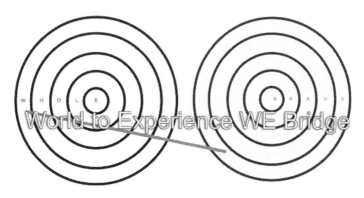

individual at the experience of the connection. This process will be quite new, especially to the relatively new BRAVE individuals.

W--E

So many usually operate, as we discussed before in the reactive mode. Thus, as we have shown you, this is where the WE experience creates a new opportunity for building the bridges. You, as a WHOLE BRAVE individual, get to show up and invite someone into the labyrinth, the circle, and the authentic experience we all want to ultimately experience.

The Bridge to connect on the first layer is taking the time to ask questions related to the first layer of their own perceptions of the world in its state today. Now, in the 2020s this is a whole new perspective. As you also learned, perspective is in the eye of the beholder. Your opportunity is to learn to listen, hear and confirm your understanding. The message you give back is, "This is what I heard you say—tell me more about this—" You will start to watch each person you walk through each of these layers with in this style slowly start to release a bit of their guard. Some individuals may need to do this one simple conversation at a time.

One other item to remember at this very sensitive time is to not to attempt to move them over to your side of the bridge. It is so easy for us at each of these layers to want someone to see all of our conversations from our side of the bridge. Yet, we lose the opportunity to deeply root in the foundation of the bridge jumping from side to side too quickly. Most relationships have to be deeply rooted to appreciate the constant jumping from side to side without any damage to the bridges. A major example of this visual I want to share with you next.

HISTORY TO VALUES

The next bridge of History to Values has a very tangible physical experience to share how this showed up in quite a few coaching examples. The first one, a couple I got to coach years ago trusted me enough to take them on a walk in a very public park. They had given me an idea to help them physically and tangibly see how they were damaging their relationship bridge. I am asking you to not practice this on your own without my supervision.

I literally glued a jump rope to two bowls with ten gel rocks in each of their bowls. WE walked through the park with the jump rope wrapped around them both. They got to walk as they guided each other to do so. They exchanged rocks as they were directed based on items we were coaching them around.

The moment it became very evident for both of them was

Building the BRIDGE

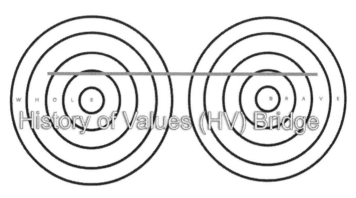

History of Values (HV) Bridge

when the wife hid her bowl and pulled as far away as she could from one specific attempt to cross the verbal bridge. She went into immediate guard for a multitude of reasons knowing this is how she responded every time this particular instant was raised. The husband had no idea this was happening in this visual way, and it opened up lots of opportunities for growth.

And, yes, we had a great deal of individuals stopping us and asking what we were doing.

The Yoked exercise worked so well we did it with a few different products at our annual summit in Monterey, California, that year. The participants were also awed by the visual representation of how easily it is to affect the other individual they are attempting to build a bridge with. Meanwhile, the biggest moment came when one team shared how much they saw each person was attempting to take control and not asking for help.

Another team that got paired up in Monterey, Califonia also got to see this experience deeply lived out. They were both alpha leaders attempting to take their own roles. As each pebble was requested to be shared, overall it all went well until one request was to have one team member dump all the pebbles in the other's bucket. The looks on both of their faces was priceless.

These makeshift bridges are very real pathways and the visual connection—whether it be a pathway, a rope, a string, or whatever it is for you and your connection—take this seriously. Some moments and damaged bridges are very difficult to mend or repair. Take time to listen, connect, and truly understand. Also understand that at some point the other party will need to do the same as no relationship should be one sided. It is a two-way path because most all relationships we are discussing ideally are partnerships.

Going back to the couples story, each pebble in their bucket represented different areas of their WHOLE and BRAVE. We get to determine how and who we perceive the buckets and pebbles are attached in each of our journeys in our history and values. We also get to determine how to share them as we choose how to walk across each bridge literally or figuratively.

More often than not, most expect the other person to walk the full length of the bridge. We get to show each other as we work to cross each other's bridges the value of our initiative. We also get to show how much we value each other when we choose to take the time to discover how they will invite us to cross through their layers and meet them where they are ready to be connected.

ORGANIZE TO ATTRACT

Ideally, we learn how to create experiences from the inside out, and we realize how we organize our stories to attract people and opportunities. We show up BEing the BRAVE we choose to BE. Who did you decide to BE? How often do you see yourself show up as that individual? What does it look like to BE imperfectly you? How do you desire people to experience you? Remembering your experience is the highest value and impacts others when you are deeply and authentically living unlayered.

The value exchanges in each relationship is challenged often because everyone has a different set of filters and lens they create value through. Our history, even an experience from yesterday, creates a historical reference point. A few of my clients refer to them as data points. Some may attempt

Building the BRIDGE

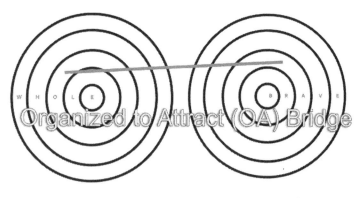

to align these data points to determine what results or beliefs they want to attach to any experience and how they will attach value. This will also determine the value they give to a relationship and the way they store the history or data they attached to the moment. The way we see this happen is as simple as when we are in a waiting room or at a restaurant. A conversation comes up, and all of a sudden, you end up in a deeper conversation because you both found some type of value exchange. In some cases, you might even create a relationship and connection.

This happens for me quite regularly and last week was another intense example. I got the gift to share a valuable relationship exchange with a beautiful soul sitting outside a dealership. We started over an appreciation for the shirt she was wearing. It was a happy place for both of us to start the conversation. As we dug in later she helped me remember a story. I had not realized how long since I had told the story, and I helped her see people are still willing to have deep conversations, even sitting waiting for our vehicles. I thanked her for her time.

The story that best deeply and graphically represents another person crossing a bridge and stepping into another person's world is this one. Yet, I realized I had forgotten about it as I told it the same morning. I had stayed up most of the night picking my son up from being kidnapped. We did not talk about any of the incident with our TrailBlazer Summit attendees because my truck had been impounded, and it was not public knowledge yet as they were still searching for the aggressors. Thankfully they are both in prison now, and one is convicted. I was in recovery mode and had stored this story away with the incident. Our conversation caused it to resurface and just for this additional awareness for us to share.

A couple bought a recovery home for young teens who no one else wanted. They had a heart for helping these young people discover how valuable and loved they were even when they felt that no one else wanted them. A young girl was a new resident. She was shown her room and given the evening to rest and told her nurse would be in to check on her in the morning. The next morning the nurse came in to find excrement all over the walls. The nurse walked back out and returned shortly after with two sets of gloves.

She said to the young girl, "Let's clean this up together." The nurse added, "If you feel you must do this, would you please consider just this wall as we will be cleaning it together as often as you need."

This continued for days if not weeks until one day the young girl finally was willing to ask the nurse, "Do you know why I need to do this?"

The nurse said, "I figured when you were ready you would share."

The young girl shared, "When my father raped me over and over again, I just felt I had to put up with it for my family. Eventually one day I crapped, and he was so disgusted he left my room. I learned that if I pooped he would go away."

This disgusting and sad example reminds us of the crap and fertilizer we discussed in our jail cells. She was living in her own jail cell, and a kind hearted nurse took time to get in the crap with her to help her see that not everyone would run away and how to start considering another option to feel safe and secure. The nurse helped her work through her history layer to see how she had organized her experience. They both also discovered they could start on a new layer once they could gain some trust, respect, and care to communicate in the way this young girl needed to be met.

I told this story at the beginning of my last TrailBlazer Summit—although at the time I didn't realize it would be my last—to help others preparing to hear the speakers. They had a choice of what they heard and where they chose to show up for others in their lives. Looking back now, I am beyond thankful for all the speakers and sponsors that weekend who helped my son and I get through an extremely traumatic experience. Overall, the final comment from one of our participants was, "No one is doing this type of work, and I am so thankful I came." We have discovered it was time to close that chapter and begin the Living Unlayered Experiences. Yet, this story is one more reminder of why it is so deeply important to build bridges, remove layers, and meet people we care about where they are.

Recalling the five people we surround ourselves with, these are the people we attract into our lives and we get to live out experiences with them by choice. We may not realize why or even how we chose some of the people we surround ourselves with. Somehow these people are being attracted to you for what you need right now. At some point in time, life circumstances may change, and you will determine how to create more space or distance and attract new people. This usually happens when the value exchange process changes in the relationship and one or the other goes a different direction. If the other does not follow this direction, they eventually will distance themselves from the relationship and find value exchanges in other relationships. This is a very deep matter in many relationships. Communicating values and direction is intensely important in any relationship.

How do we organize this understanding? For me, movies have a tendency to come up with visual examples. Jim Carry, who plays Bruce, in *Bruce Almighty* is the movie that immediately popped into my mind. He gets to meet Morgan Freeman, who is playing God in this movie. They are in a white warehouse, and God and Bruce are having a conversation about all the moments of Bruce's life. Bruce doesn't seem to think too much about this conversation until the moment the file cabinet is opened. If you remember this movie you may see this hilarious part in your mind. The file cabinet literally sends Bruce across the warehouse as he is holding on to the file drawer realizing he has much more stored than he realized. God pulls the file out he wants and knocks on the file cabinet to return it to his closed position bringing Bruce quickly across the room again.

As one of my mentors would say, we have two file sources stored in the same file cabinet, and we get to decide which approach we take to open the cabinet. We get to decide if we want to pull the failures or the successes. Again, fertilizer or crap? We get to choose how we filter each experience and as Morgan Freeman—God—reminds us, we have plenty to choose from.

The file cabinet we draw open we get to remember, connect, and find history is also a file cabinet we get to contribute to. Every experience gets labeled, organized, and filed into one filter or another. We get to learn day by day how to take our crap and make it fertilizer. Now that we have clarified the bridge process we personally go through in organizing and attracting, how do we cross this bridge?

How does this show up in a relationship or a conversation? The next time we have a friend we choose to spend time with

and they share about an experience, we get to ask questions.
Sample conversation:

> *Friend: "My family have a property they must get ready to sell immediately. They are overwhelmed, challenged with contractors, and we all feel like it won't get done in time."*

> *We respond: "Wow, it sounds like a great deal of stress for your family, how are you feeling in the midst of all of this?"*

> *(Note for many Realtors or fix it people, like myself, a 20 year veteran, who is a referral agent only now, this is not time to go into fix it mode or jump layers. The gift we are giving our friend at this moment is the ability to feel heard and help them organize their thoughts and in some cases just remind them to breathe.)*

> *Friend: "After you get a moment to breathe, tell me about a time when have you experienced something similar to this and overcame the circumstances?"*

(Of course, this could be phrased differently, yet if someone has the bandwidth of brain space, they may need to bring out a file of success or feeling empowered.)

As they answer, they may feel like this is just another time constraint and they will change subjects or some even prefer to stay in stress mode or victim in some circumstances. Another option is to ask what options they have considered which helps an individual work on how they are organizing and attracting what they need.

We get to stay in our BRAVE place as we are finding a middle ground in the relationship value exchange and meeting somewhere on the bridge. Guiding a WHOLE person into their layers of history, organization, and into the deeper layers of love and responsibility may require even more patience. Choosing to be responsible and see the immense gifts we can share with people walking inside their layers with them is an act of love, sometimes even from a distance.

Our core experiences in these deeper layers all have their own landmines. All the layers truly have their own triggers, and many at some point in time realize they have been hiding in their outside layers to avoid the depth of the inside layers.

LOVE TO RESPONSIBILITY

The love layer has so many layers with so many attachments to it. Thus, when a BRAVE, responsible heart works to cross a bridge and make a WHOLE connection it is possible to get blocked with triggers and armory. In a Diversity, Equity, and Inclusion lesson I created and get to teach, I share a teeter-totter of perceptions and reminders that we have landmines everywhere. Due to so many perceptions these

Building the BRIDGE

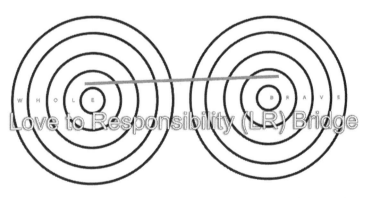

landmines got laid long before we attempted to cross the bridge. Sadly, many get blown up figuratively and even help the FEAR inside a person create another landmine.

In our world, this shows up in politics, religion, race, class, and so much more. Our so-called love of something becomes a division of someone else's love of something. We create identities and experiences that get attached to what we love. In some cases, when we attempt to see another perspective, it may make us feel like we are violating a person or memory by choosing to consider a new perspective. It would require us to let go of an attachment. In some worlds, cultures, and families that is their way of life. I remember a client releasing my services when they realized what we were working on would not align with her families and cultural beliefs. Her higher priority of family and cultural norms became more important than anything she thought she wanted or needed. We do get to choose, even if we choose to not choose. Every choice has its consequences and rewards.

How do we begin to have these conversations? We get to cross the bridge tenderly, reminding ourselves there are many landmines even when you are invited into the layer. What we love we are deeply connected to! Here is an example of a simple non-heated conversation.

> *Friend: "I love gardening."*
> *We respond: "What do you love about it most?"*
> *Friend: "The seeds becoming a plant, the flowers blooming, and all the different types of plants and flowers."*
> *We respond: "It sounds like gardening has lots of options and life cycles and they really matter to you. When did you start gardening or what made it so enjoyable for you?"*

Friend: "My grandmother really took a lot of time to help me understand all the beauty in the planting process. She showed me the ways to help the plants grow and the insect challenges that could intrude in the process"

We respond: "A lot of life could resemble that thought, have you seen any of those lessons play out in other areas of your life?"

This is where the responsibility to dig a little deeper could be hit with a roadblock or trigger and depending on how much relationship we have it will require the brain, heart, and soul to align to go deeper into a core thought.

Remember this is scary stuff for everyone at times. Walking inside our onion, layer by layer, helping another person walk inside their own onion is a process. Guiding conversations to walk inside layers is also scary stuff. Once you invite someone in, it is not wise to kick them back out. Once we give someone permission to walk inside our layers, they have now left a mark, an indent, and sometimes even a gift.

The BE is the depth of the core layer and, in my opinion, is best described in a labyrinth experience we will discuss in the next chapter.

SUMMARY

In a recent bridge building experience, I fell short and did exactly what I wrote about to *not* do. I crossed the bridge too quickly, and it blew up!

I took a step back knowing it would be great material for the book of course and a wonderful human learning experience. There was a multitude of conversations that dominoed each other.

One of those lessons was discovering an equation I created years ago that I was finally able to understand because the person on the other end of the conversation wanted data points for their value exchange.

This equation will get shared in detail in our next chapter, yet it helped me discover another way to mend a bridge and determine a better way to build.

All of us get in a hurry at times, fall short, in our own ability to slay one layer at a time. Our worldly bridge experiences open us up to opportunities.

If we historically value these conversations and connections, we get to build the next bridge of organizing and attracting evidence to clarify how we want to invite someone into the next layer or not.

The deeper layers is where our BRAVE love and responsibility builds deeper bridges. We daily get to choose to stay out of victim which is difficult even for experienced bridge builders.

We get to choose to see each other accurately as one of my coaches reminded me and many other coaches from our Habit Finder community. This is where we ultimately get to learn to trust oursselves.

We get to BE present in each Experience. For those spiritually interested and/or curious you will want to deep dive into the next chapter. Feel free to keep repeating experiences as you choose as well!

LIVING UNLAYERED CHAPTER FIVE COMMITMENTS

- My commitment is to meet each person where they are!
- My commitment is to invite each person to cross a bridge with me as they are ready!
- My commitment is to gently and kindly ask questions to discover where the other bridge builder is on the bridge!
- My commitment is to understand and empathize without internalizing!
- My commitment is to value and share!
- My commitment is to clarify which file drawer I am choosing to open!
- I choose to continue to engage in the Onion Slayer community to encourage and BE encourage!

CHAPTER SIX

THE LABYRINTH EXPERIENCE
WHERE THE HEART, SOUL, AND MIND CONNECT

"With a labyrinth, you make a choice to go in—and once you've chosen, around and around you go. But you always find your way to the center."

~Jeff Bridges

Many see a labyrinth as a meditation exercise, I see it as a spiritual experience. I had a wise leader share this location with my daughter which made me want to explore it and learn about labyrinths. The Alta Sierra Biblical Garden was

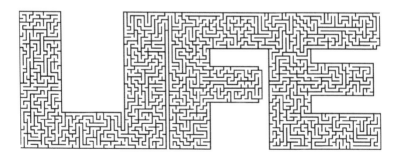

my first experience with a labyrinth. It was also a place I got to go for my Spiritual Disciplines class and take many others through the same location. One specific experience helped me start seeing the opportunity to include this experience in my TrailBlazer Summit, as well as with you.

It was my first launch of the Masters League Competition in 2018 where we met in person at the Roseville Area Chamber conference room. We were deep into the WHOLE and BRAVE lessons where it hit my girlfriend hard. She was taking the course as an author who had launched her own book. She realized she was a small business owner with her book and wanted to learn how to promote it better. There was a conversation that came up that challenged her and I offered for us to take the afternoon off and take it to a spiritual experience. We did and went to the Biblical Gardens. It was on this day I saw the WHOLE and BRAVE in the labyrinth.

Our world teaches us to live in the exterior layers. Choosing to look in the mirror, walk inside ourselves, is an extremely deep choice and counterintuitive to small talk. Choosing to surrender our heart, mind, and soul to a source beyond ourselves is even deeper. Each of our labyrinth experiences are more than just a physical walk through a garden. There is a mental, emotional, and spiritual process that gives us the opportunity to invite the Holy Spirit within us and within the walk. Inviting God in any type of walk is a form of surrender and quiet leadership.

Years ago, I asked a leader I was interviewing if she saw me as a quiet leader, she abruptly and positively responded with "No!" I thanked her for her perception and asked her if she understood quiet leadership. She didn't realize then

I saw her as one of my future leaders of the 85 people who would end up on my coaching roster in the Palmdale real estate office I got to set records in with the powerful team we aligned. She didn't realize that if I would have come in steam rolling into the office a previous coach left, I would have been kicked out the minute I got there.

I realized people needed to get to know me, mourn the loss of the coach they all deeply loved, and watch me lead by example. Through interviewing, connecting, and deep diving I earned the respect of 85 people who chose me as their coach. In 10 months we shocked everyone with our results from our vision to have explosive results. It really showed when we had a Christmas party and we played musical chairs—that old party game where the music is played and a chair gets taken away each song. It was down to the broker of the office—a very strong personality—and myself. We had to grab items from the people in the audience before landing back in our chair. I want to say it came down to a sock, and I was blessed to grab it first. If I remember correctly, no one would give my competition the sock until I got back to my chair. I came into the office the next week, and many people said to me, "If you could beat her, you belong here!"

There were so many personalities in the 400-agent office, I got to learn how to show up strong for some, considerate and compassionate for others, and ultimately walk inside the labyrinth of the culture of the office I got to lead. The manager I worked for then called me back years later and asked me to consider coming to work for another location he now owned. He said, "You were always the glue." We ultimately didn't end up aligning again, yet his kindness to see the impact was deeply appreciated.

In every walk into any labyrinth, we get to create value relationships exchanges, and in the real estate office, I was building the WHOLE and BRAVE perspectives without anyone realizing the process we were walking through. Choosing to be silent is difficult for many. So many need so much noise to fill the space. Some are truly afraid of the noise in their heads, thus they choose a different noise to drown it out. This is especially true in high-stress situations or environments. The real estate industry and many others have a whole lot of emotion and opportunities to find peace. I was just beginning to understand all the depth of my discoveries myself.

Now we are digging deeper into the labyrinths, the heart, mind, and soul of the internal perspectives of paths we get to take. If you are willing, we may see how God guides us to know and see God living in us. Our internal labyrinth, the WHOLE and BRAVE, are tangible labyrinth layers.

When you walk a tangible labyrinth you discover the path has many directions. Once you think you are walking inside the labyrinth, it walks you back out to the outer layer. This happens in life and in crossing bridges. Some are only able to cross certain areas of the bridge, and at certain times they will escape the labyrinth experience to safe layers or what they consider safe comfort zones that are not so comfortable.

Ironically, I never thought someone would literally work to escape a literal labyrinth until one day I was walking through the one at the Biblical Gardens, and a man walked by me multiple times. Finally, after I felt he was a relatively safe and harmless soul, he approached me and shared that I reminded him of his wife he had recently lost who loved to walk the labyrinth. He shared they would visit the garden often, yet he would not walk the labyrinth. He said he was personally afraid of it, and even when I offered to walk it with him, he did literally escape from my presence. It almost seemed as if the labyrinth represented so much more than the man knew how to express. It still makes me wonder today, how many others are afraid of any type of labyrinth?

For our slaying the onion and living unlayered experience, let's believe we are all willing participants in all senses. For those looking for a physical labyrinth, visit *https://labyrinthlocator.com*. Make sure to verify with the location all the details before venturing out to a location. There are a multitude of ways to experience a labyrinth. For our purposes, in all perspectives, physical, emotional, mental, and spiritual let's go back to your experiences with the life wheel, the WHOLE experience, and BRAVE, and especially the jail cells! Each of these journeys ideally revealed some layers. We all have a multitude of layers.

Before you begin to attempt to tackle all the layers at once, we will take them one layer at a time. What I have also discovered over the years is there is usually an overarching theme. Almost every week all my recurring clients seem to have a theme that rises up for each and every one of them for the week. This may ring true in this journey. As you have been doing the digging, slaying, and journaling, what theme have you seen rise up over and over again?

Today, as I walked the labyrinth again and wrote part of this chapter in the center of it, I realized my theme continues to be in each and every experience how am I letting God BE daily present in my life. It takes me back to the first time I was woken out of a deep sleep and told the Pastor was going to call on me in church. Not everyone has had the

101

experience of God speaking to them, and I do not consider myself the only one that has ever happened to, yet I do hear it can be rare.

A friend who attended that church with me was in a small group with me recently and shared she remembered the pastor calling on me. I was in a season of learning God was the center of my puzzle, and I was learning how to be on fire without burning anyone to share God's love. The pastor said to the congregation, "You want to watch someone grow from a mustard seed to a large tree with tons of shade, watch how God will work in this woman's life."

Just like the day my real estate broker said to me in a rough tone, "You are just another Steven Covey," I didn't realize at the moment the depth of these prophecies. We are our own worst enemies. God has wanted to use me in a mighty way and does consistently in the areas I surrender myself too.

Recently I have known I am being called to the next stage. As I walked through the labyrinth I heard the pastor at Faith Promise remind me that God's favor stays for an obedient soul. I do not ever want to take God's favor for granted. Being obedient means we get to bring everything to the storehouse and let God transform it all. It is always better than anything we do in our power. I am human just like everyone, and I am a work in progress everyday.

Yet, when my singles minister gave all of the leaders the book, *Master Plan of Evangelism*, I took it to heart and read every word. One particular quote stood out!

"No one knew better than Jesus that the Satanic forces of darkness against them were well organized and equipped to make ineffectual any half-hearted effort of evangelism. They

*could not possibly outwit the devilish powers of this world
unless they gave strict adherence to him who alone knew the
strategy of victory. This required obedience to the Master's
will, even if it meant complete abondonment of their own!"*
                                    ~*Master Plan of Evangelism*, pg 58

This is why I know the next stage requires all of my obedience.
One of the obedience items of many God is working on
me is tithing, and ironically my monthly tithe was unable to
go through today. It wouldn't process. There was no tangible
reason for it to be stopped as funds were available. The super-
natural reason was God getting my attention. I truly knew
God was telling me it was time to step it up. It reminded
me of a season where I was serving two masters. I was a six
figure real estate agent with two personal assistants—one
who was teaching my daughter to shoplift, drink vodka in
her water bottle, and smoke marijuana in my backyard while
I was working to pay her. Needless to say, she was released,
and many other challenges were faced at this time.

As I mentioned previously, in a recent divine connection,
a Bridge Builder was an equation person. Realizing I had
jumped a few layers in our conversations too quickly, the Holy
Spirit helped me remember an equation I wrote years ago.

It was July 8/9th at 12:10 a.m. that this equation got
inspired in my notes. FREE Will = Choices + Education
multiplied by Faith divided by Exhalted Prayer equals Divine
Revelation.

It hit me as I was connecting the process over the years
my FREE Will is the Radar and Layers, the Choices is
what I chose responsibility for, and the Education is what I
organized or attracted to support those choices. My Faith is

completely connected to my belief and trust in my love and responsibility to myself, and others and the Exhalted Prayer was my commitment to ask for and celebrate the values and experiences.

All of these discoveries have been part of the paths the Holy Spirit wanted to lead each of us on. It still shocks me how often I get to get remind myself and other believers to connect, listen, and value the Holy Spirit.

In my season four solocast of our podcast takes me almost 20 minutes to get to the root of how important this reminder is. Yet, when I remember when I was a new believer I had to remind myself, "Many do not have ears to hear and eyes to see."

If that is you right now or you need a refresher opportunity to remember how to hear the Holy Spirit, how to connect and establish a personal relationship with the redeemer, I personally know named Jesus Christ. Let me invite you today.

Let God and I take this precious moment right here and now to invite you into a personal relationship with Christ. There is nothing you have to do or prepare for to receive the gift of our Holy Heavenly Redeemer to love you unconditionally!

This is a simple we all pray together pray every Sunday at my church, Faith Promise in Knoxville, Tennessee. I will pray it with you right now with my own personal flair.

Dear Precious God, I want a new life, I want a new heart, as in Ezekiel 36:26 shares you will give me a new heart.

I am a sinner and I thank you for sending your son, Christ to die on a Christ for my sins.

I want a personal relationship with you right now. I surrender my will and pray to have the Holy Spirit come into my life!

*I pray to get to know you more and more every day. Give
me the ears to hear your precious words, the eyes to see your
precious miracles, and the new heart to recieve your love.*

In Jesus Name, we pray!

Praise God! This is literally the first time I have truly ever
gotten the opportunity to walk a new believer into an invitation to cross this type of bridge! I pray we have earned the
trust and refreshing gift of a renewed heart for you!

I pray you can now see what a Spiritual, Mental, Emotional,
and Physical labryinth begins to look like as we journey into
the core of your beliefs, your layers and you future paths.

Thank you for trusting yourself to slay through your layers.
Thank you Lord for walking with us on this incredibly
precious journey. God the father, Christ the Son, and The
gift of the Holy Spirit create the trinity we celebrate in
this moment.

All believers in our Slaying the Onion and Living Unlayered community want to celebrate with you. Let me also
remind you that there may still be hearts that do not hear
yet and eyes that do not see yet that are still learning. Have
grace with us!

This was truly my divine revelation of this whole book
was to get to be the vessel for you. Yes, you! We each get to
be obedient to when God tells us to touch a life, and I was
editing this chapter when I realized it was time to give this
invitation.

I asked my publisher for another weekend to add many
missing items in the book, and this was the biggest one I now
know that I was called to share. It was because God wanted
you to know He truly wants you to experience a BRAVE
personal relationship.

105

SUMMARY

God taught me so many lessons and made me remember what it was to look for milk money in the couches. The biggest lesson was where my BE came from. Being present in God's presence, Being present as completely without wrinkles or stains, no matter how many mistakes you have made, being present, loved and valued by your creator and then by yourself is a journey. Knowing there is absolutely nothing you have to do to earn this love and nothing will ever take it away from you—this is LOVE.

The other memory I had as I walked today was of the Christian Rock band on the Dollywood stage recently who showed up to completely honor God. Every ounce of their presentation was all about glorifying God. I knew when I could completely take a stage with that immense laser focus is when the doors would open to speak and impact even more lives. The world operates on one set of expectations which is why the WHOLE experience is understanding your perception of the external world and the internal world. They are two different experiences.

The pastor reminded me that God does not need my money. A God-fearing church doesn't need my money, neither does any other ministry I give to. What God wants is my complete obedience and trust in what He promises me. I get to actively worship through my tithing, serving, and using my gifts on whatever stage He calls me to next.

Over the years, God has been working on me in understanding value, releasing self-sacrifice, giving me permission to earn a profit with key sharing of funds. God's favor is available for all of us in His time and His way. I am not skilled to understand and explain it all. What I am skilled to do is share my testimony. I have gone as Paul with none and learned to be content, and I have known the gift of being blessed abundantly to bless others. Through the journey I have walked many forms of labyrinths and am now learning how to inspire others to do the same.

Now is just us, and I am asking you to hear, feel and experience every ounce of this message! It will seem strange to hear and even more powerful to feel, yet your heart, mind, and soul matter to me and matter to God. Your labyrinth experience is God walking with you. The onions you are slaying are all part of this journey. We truly feel your pain, your joy, and your desires to step into the BRAVE soul you are intended to BE and are called to BE. It is possible!

God willing you are in our community, taking the online course, and if you are able to experience a living unlayered experience near you. We are just getting started, and we need you! We all have many layers to slay and many to help learn how. We get to make fertilizer out of crap, we get to help people out of their jail cells, and we get to slay our onions! This is where we go into Next Steps!

Living Unlayered Chapter Six Commitments

- I choose to learn and understand my spiritual, emotional, and physical labyrinths.
- I choose to be obedient to the Holy Spirit!
- I choose to remove any half-hearted efforts!
- I choose to align my choices, education, multiplying my faith in exalted prayer!
- I choose to share my testimony trusting God with how it will be received!
- I choose to be a vessel to guide others into a personal relationship with God!
- I choose to go to all nations making disciples!

CHAPTER SEVEN

NEXT STEPS

Once you make a decision, the universe conspires to make it happen.

~Ralph Waldo Emerson

Wow, what a journey we have been on. Now that we ideally have walked through your radar and life wheel, been through the WHOLE experience, removed a few jail cells, dove into the BRAVE experience, built a few bridges including a walk into a labryinth, what could possibly be next? This is the journey I have been on determining how I may walk with you in every step of this journey.

When I approached the owner who created a position for me, I told him, "I have been the jack-of-all-trades—I want to be a Master of Coaching." He didn't really know what that meant and—as I learned—neither did I. A few years later, as a coach running my own business, I realized that leadership was truly the missing layer. Thus, I chose to get a Masters in Biblical Leadership. It took many units in personal, professional, and biblical leadership to earn our Masters Degree. A few quotes I shared in my personal reflection of myself as a leader are included in our *what's next* process. Slaying the Onion doesn't end when you finish this book. Realistically, you may revisit these exercises as often as you want to.

> *"If there is one thing leaders need as they pursue self knowledge is the ability to clarify their fears, motives, insecurities, and other emotions that lurk deep beneath the surface of their public persona"*
>
> ~Rima, p. 142

We all get to daily and deeply discover the BE within ourselves beyond all the distractions and noise. We get to BE responsible, attracting, and creating valuable relationships, exchanges, and experiences. Meeting another person where they are, patiently and kindly earning the invitation into their layers, is the gift we get to share as we learn how to build bridges.

> *"In fact, connecting with the reality of our Calling in a meaningful way is the key that will unlock for us a life enduring significance and purpose that informs every other activity in which we engage."*
>
> ~Rima, 2000

It is a wonderful gift to know we don't need to be perfect. It is also a wonderful gift to know what areas in our leadership we have opportunity to grow.

> *"When we make it through the Wall, we no longer have a need to be well known or successful, but to do God's will."*
>
> ~Scazzero, 2006

As in most churches and organizations, there is always a process for next steps. At Faith Promise Pastor Chris Stephens deeply got my attention when he filmed one of his *next steps* videos from Brushy prison inside one of the jail cells. It literally made me know I needed to go and personally experience it as I share in the jail cells chapter. The clarity he shared to remind each and every person listening was, we all have a choice to remove ourselves from our prisons. I pray I too have duplicated and added additional value to this message.

I get to let God work through me as we discover what this means for you. We get to serve obediently to honor and glorify God. When we make it about us and remove God from first position, then we face other obstacles and concerns.

"Your attitude should be the same as that of Christ Jesus."
~Phil 2:5 (NIV)

"It is God who works in you to will and act according to his good purpose."
~Phil 2:13 (NIV)

This verse was taught to me by my first life coach to what I was given the gift to do in coaching with others through the Holy Spirit. God will work through us in our obedience. Only when you are ready, truly done the deep dives and willing to create space for a group would you want to consider taking on a group and leading them through these experiences as a whole. It will require a new layer you may not see coming. I'm not saying God won't walk you and I through all the things we didn't see coming. Yet, sometimes it is worth walking a path in advance of someone you are leading in order to see some areas of landmines you experience and may want to give some insight into.

What we have found over and over again, the more you do the exercises, then as you walk someone else through the exercises, and even walking a labyrinth with you, the layers become more and more revealed. For some who have done some work already, these exercises and processes just add to the joy of self discovery. For some who have not done any work, get in community, listen to the online course, and feel free to reach out for additional support locally or from us. We know this slaying process is much deeper than most would admit to immediately.

SUMMARY

Slaying the Onion is a layer by layer, story by story experience to reveal your highest potential. There is no limit to this journey while we are all here on this earth. There are a multitude of ways to add air to your tires or life wheel, peel additional layers, and ultimately take the WHOLE BRAVE bridge experiences into your divine revelation equations.

I trust the Holy Spirit as we are closing this chapter I know we have said all we need to say for now. Thankfully, my publisher reminded me we may add edits as needed . Yet, most importantly Onion Slayer to Onion Slayer, it is my prayer that our commitment to live unlayered every day gives others permission to do the same. Be the light to inspire other lights to shine. Remember you have an unique fingerprint to make an unique imprint. Keep slaying to shine at your highest potential!

Living Unlayered Chapter Seven Commitments

- Living Unlayered means one unveiled layer at a time!
- Living Unlayered means I invite myself and others to know what matters on my radar!
- Living Unlayered means I take time to know my WHOLE self!
- Living Unlayered means I remove jail cells!
- Living Unlayered means I show up BRAVE in my highest potential!
- Living Unlayered means my labyrinth experience creates divine revelations!
- Living Unlayered means I connect with others to take my next steps!

References

Coleman, R. E. (1964). *The master plan of evangelism.* Westwood, NJ: F.H. Revell.

Gomez, D (2009). *The heart of a leader: Connecting leading and the inner life.* Inner Resources for Leaders. Retrieved from http://www.regent.edu/acad/global/publications/innerresources/vol1iss1/gomez_innerlife.pdf

Holy Bible ESV Bible. (2016). Crossway Books.

Rima, S. (2000). *Leading from the inside out.* Grand Rapids, MI: Baker Book House

Scazzero, P. (2006). *Emotionally healthy spirituality.* Grand Rapids, MI: Baker Book House

The Holy Bible: New international version, containing the Old Testament and the New Testament. (1978). Grand Rapids: Zondervan Bible.

Blanchard, D. (2012) *Today I Begin a New Life,* Og Press

Heifetz, R.A. & Linsky, M. (2002) *Leadership on the Line: Staying Alive Through the Dangers of Leading,* MA:Harvard Business School Press

Flint, R (2004) *The Truth About Stress: Understanding your Life from the Inside Out,* Newport News, VA

Maister, D. et al *The Trusted Advisor* (2021) New York, NY

About the Author

April Diana Jean Ballestero—author, coach, consultant, guide—secured her Masters degree in Biblical Leadership and her Bachelors degree in Vocational Education. She is Habit Finder certified from Og Mandino Leadership, Abelson DISC certified, is a Master Graduate from Rapport Leadership International, and previously served as Regional Occupational Teacher at San Juan School District for real estate course.

April's majority focus for the last three decades has been and continues to be empowering, inspiring, and guiding light bulb moments.

Connect with April ∼ **Access the Course**

Made in the USA
Columbia, SC
16 October 2021